T0199086

The Crown Has Fallen

A Study of the Kings of Judah

Marty McLain

WESTBOW
PRESS®
A DIVISION OF THOMAS NELSON
& ZONDERVAN

This book is a work of non-fiction. Unless otherwise noted, the author and the publisher make no explicit guarantees as to the accuracy of the information contained in this book and in some cases, names of people and places have been altered to protect their privacy.

WestBow Press books may be ordered through booksellers or by contacting:

WestBow Press
A Division of Thomas Nelson & Zondervan
1663 Liberty Drive
Bloomington, IN 47403
www.westbowpress.com
1 (866) 928-1240

Scripture taken from the New King James Version®. Copyright © 1982 by Thomas Nelson. Used by permission. All rights reserved.

ISBN: 978-1-9736-6111-5 (sc)
ISBN: 978-1-9736-6113-9 (hc)
ISBN: 978-1-9736-6112-2 (e)

Library of Congress Control Number: 2019907072

Print information available on the last page.

WestBow Press rev. date: 06/10/2019

An Onion by
Any Other Name

I grew up in the South Georgia town of Vidalia. My coming of age was in the 1980s, which in retrospect seemed to be the ideal time to live in small-town America. The international trade deals had not yet gutted the lion's share of American manufacturing jobs, and the internet had not yet been made publicly available. Life was lived on a local level. Ronald Reagan was president. Pro wrestling was still big, and O. J. Simpson was still my hero. It seemed that every town had its own claim to fame. Claxton had its fruitcakes. Reidsville had the prison, and Vidalia had the onions.

During the 1980s, the Vidalia onion was coming into its own. In 1980, none other than the *Wall Street Journal* referred to the Vidalia onion as "the caviar of onions."[1] The popularity of the onion continued to spread so much that in 1986, the Georgia General Assembly passed legislation defining a twenty-county Vidalia onion growing region. This designation would help to protect the integrity of the product. It seems that the secret to

---

[1] https://newspaperarchive.com/walla-walla-union-bulletin-jul-13-1980-p-1/.

the sweet onion lies not only in the type of seed planted but also in a combination of climate and soil.[2] Three years after the General Assembly's action, the federal government got involved by enacting Federal Marketing Order No. 955, which provided federal protection for the Vidalia onion.[3] Additionally, in 1990, the state legislature declared the Vidalia onion to be the state vegetable, and in 1992, the state of Georgia became the owner of the Vidalia onion trademark.[4] The lucrative crop was protected by force of law.

However, the protection of the integrity of the Vidalia onion required constant diligence. Take, for instance, two rather high-profile cases. Delbert Bland, owner of one of the oldest and largest onion farms, was taken to court in 2014 for selling his crop of Vidalia onions before the official release date. Some contend that harvesting onions too soon can adversely affect the quality of the product. To prevent damage to the reputation of the onion, it had been determined that the head of the Georgia Department of Agriculture should decide the date when the onions can go to market. Failure to observe the release date can result in a substantial fine.[5] The court case drew national attention and even the legal services of one of Georgia's former attorneys general.

Perhaps the most intriguing case occurred in 2015, when a

---

[2] https://www.nytimes.com/2014/04/09/dining/vidalia-onions-a-crop-with-an-image-to-uphold.html.

[3] https://www.vidaliaonions.com/history/.

[4] https://georgiainfo.galileo.usg.edu/topics/history/article/fdrs.../vidalia-onions.

[5] http://www.sandiegouniontribune.com/sdut-vidalia-onion-farmer-back-in-court-over-ship-date-2014apr14-story.html#.

Vidalia onion farm owned by billionaire Bill Gates was suspected of mixing onions from a Florida farm with Vidalia onions. Discovery of the potential breach of law led to a nighttime meeting with the state agricultural commissioner and local farmers.[6] Eventually, it was determined that no illegitimate onions were sold as Vidalia onions. However, rules pertaining to handling the onions were violated. During the investigation, $100,000 worth of onions spoiled. This loss was deemed as a sufficient fine for the transgression of one of the world's richest men.[7] The onion must be protected at all costs.

Just as the South Georgia farmers must protect the reputation of the Vidalia onion, the God of the Bible is even more heavily invested in the protection of His name through the actions of His people. God has a reputation on this earth that He puts in the hands of those who bear His name. Second Corinthians 5:20 says that Christians are "ambassadors for Christ." In Acts 1:8, Jesus says His followers are His "witnesses" on this earth. First Corinthians 12:27 declares that believers make up the "body of Christ" on this earth. As such, God's reputation must be protected much like the Vidalia onion is protected. The quality of the product affects its value in the eyes of the consumers. God's reputation is either enhanced or diminished by His people. The same can be said about the Jews in the Old Testament.

---

[6] http://www.onlineathens.com/business/2015-08-08/bill-gates-foiled-georgias-powerful-vidalia-onion-regulators.

[7] https://politics.myajc.com/blog/politics/billionaire-bill-gates-runs-afoul-georgia-vidalia-onion-police/Yq9PxyGWr1Nkp4dsMTQsnL/.

God's Chosen People

In the Old Testament, God called a man named Abraham into a special relationship with Him. Out of all the people in the ancient world, God spoke these words to this man who dwelt in Mesopotamia:

> Get out of your country, from your family and from your father's house, to a land that I will show you. I will make you a great nation; I will bless you and make your name great; and you shall be a blessing. I will bless those who bless you and I will curse him who curses you; and in you all the families of the earth shall be blessed. (Genesis 12:1–3)

God was going to bless Abraham and his descendants in such a way that all the world would be blessed. Of course, Abraham would be the father of the Jewish nation. His descendants would spend four hundred years in Egyptian slavery before they would be brought out by a deliverer named Moses. Another leader, Joshua, would guide them into the Promised Land, where they would be ruled by a series of judges, such as Gideon and Samson. The Jews would eventually transition into a monarchy, with the descendants of King David sitting on the throne in Jerusalem. The Davidic kingdom would experience a devastating split, with ten of the twelve tribes breaking off to form a new nation in the north. The northern kingdom, as it would become known, was given to idolatry from the start, and it eventually experienced a brutal end at the hands of the Assyrian Empire in 721 BC.

The southern kingdom, also known as Judah, was fortunate to continue the Davidic lineage of kings. Some of the kings were good, and others were terrible. The Jewish nation tended to drift in the direction of the king's spiritual condition. Even the good kings tended to have a tragic flaw that prevented them from finishing well. At times, these kings demonstrated incredible faith as they navigated the challenges they faced. At other times, they showed an unfortunate tendency to mishandle their successes.

It bears remembering that God had set the Jewish nation to be a light to the Gentiles. They were to be an example to the pagan nations as to how the true God was to be known and worshipped. Unfortunately, for the most part, the Jewish nation failed miserably. Their failure eventually culminated in their defeat and dispersion at the hands of the Babylonians in 586 BC. However, just as Rome did not fall in a day, neither did Judah. The seeds of its rebellion toward God did not sprout overnight but were nurtured over centuries. The story is one from which we all can learn.

Chapter 1

Rheboam

Read 1 Kings 12–14 and 2 Chronicles 10–12.

Breaking Up Is Hard to Do

Family breakups are hard to watch. It is disheartening to observe when familial love and affection are suddenly torn apart. When families are embroiled in this level of hate, the result is years of misery and alienation. Take, for instance, Adolphus and Rudolph Dassler. These German brothers founded the Dassler Brothers Sports Shoe Company in the 1920s. This fraternal enterprise thrived even as Adolf Hitler assumed command of the German nation. These siblings were so much on the cutting edge of athletic shoes that they even got American superstar Jesse Owens to wear their product at the 1936 Olympics in Berlin.[8]

---

[8] http://fortune.com/2013/03/22/the-hatred-and-bitterness-behind-two-of-the-worlds-most-popular-brands/.

However, WWII changed everything. The Dassler brothers were already at the opposite ends of the personality spectrum. Adolphus was a shy introvert, while Rudolph was a gregarious extrovert.[9] To complicate matters further, during the war, Rudolph accused Adolphus of not wanting to share a bomb shelter with his family. The alienation intensified when, at the conclusion of the war, Adolphus confided to the Allies that his brother Rudolph was a member of the Gestapo.[10] This betrayal led to an extended postwar prison sentence for Rudolph.

Because of the tension between the brothers, they parted ways in 1948 and set up two rival shoe companies. Adolphus named his company Adidas, and Rudolph eventually named his company Puma. These two factories operated on opposite sides of the river that ran through their hometown of Herzogenaurach, Germany. It is said that the companies even divided the town, so much so that it was called "the town of bent necks" because residents would look down to see what brand of shoes someone was wearing before they would begin a conversation.[11]

It is safe to say that family breakups produce a lot of collateral damage.

---

[9] http://www.newsweek.com/history-adidas-and-puma-86373.

[10] http://fortune.com/2013/03/22/the-hatred-and-bitterness-behind-two-of-the-worlds-most-popular-brands/.

[11] https://www.cnbc.com/2013/10/09/sporting-rivals-adidas-originals-puma-herzogenaurach.html.

A Bad Inheritance

The Bible describes how the Jewish nation in the Old Testament divided up into northern and southern kingdoms. History records how the descendants of the patriarch Abraham could not stay together once they firmly established themselves in the Promised Land. The Jews had painfully transitioned from a theocracy led by judges to a monarchy led by kings. The first king, Saul, disqualified himself as a leader, and God raised up a shepherd boy named David to take his place. David prospered in spite of a few self-inflicted wounds, and then he handed the kingdom off to his son Solomon. Of course, Solomon is often referred to as the wisest fool who ever lived. He greatly expanded the kingdom, but he did not follow his own advice and at his death left behind a son who was not up to the job.

Solomon had not left a good setup for his son, Rehoboam. Despite his vast God-given wisdom, Solomon chose folly. By his own admission, he summed up his worldly pursuits in life with the words "Vanity of vanities, all is vanity" (Ecclesiastes 1:2). Solomon overmarried, and he overspent. It would be his family and his citizens who would eventually pay the price for his indulgences. Additionally, his pursuit of women led to his heart being turned away from the Lord and toward idols (1 Kings 11:4). Without a doubt, his legacy was a political and moral mixed bag.

After Solomon's death, Rehoboam came to the throne at the age of forty-one. He was the third king in the lineage of David. One commentator noted that it is usually the third generation that squanders the family wealth.[12] Rehoboam's lifestyle and decisions only serve to reinforce this notion. For years, the ten northern tribes had been feeling the heavy load of providing the lion's share of money for the monarchy. In a shrewd move, Rehoboam decided to hold his coronation in the northern town of Shechem. Perhaps this location would gloss over any issue the people had with the heavy taxation. However, this display of pomp and circumstance did not negate the northern tribes chafing under the revenuer's heavy yoke. The pocketbook is indeed a powerful motivator. It's like the phrase popularized by James Carville, former president Bill Clinton's longtime political advisor. During the run-up to the 1992 presidential election, Carville kept everyone on point with a simple phrase, "It's the economy."[13] For Rehoboam, it was taxes.

Festering resentment had created an atmosphere that was ripe for rebellion. Into this environment, an exile named Jeroboam was summoned by the people to return from Egypt. He immediately became the leader of the northern tribes. Jeroboam is not new to the story. Years earlier, a prophet named Ahijah had prophesized that Jeroboam would take the ten northern tribes and form a new kingdom (1 Kings 11:31). This tearing asunder of the Jewish kingdom was part of God's judgment on Solomon for his persistence in idolatry. The sentence would be carried out after his death. Now, as scripture predicted, Jeroboam had returned from exile to represent the ten northern tribes as they gave

---

[12] Warren Wiersbe, *Be Responsible* (Colorado Springs, CO: David C. Cook2002), 115.

[13] https://www.huffingtonpost.com/jerry-jasinowski/presidential-debates_b_8478456.html.

Rehoboam an ultimatum concerning the future. With the crowd assembled at Shechem, Jeroboam threw a bucket of cold water on the coronation festivities. As the representative of the northern tribes, he made this simple demand to Rehoboam. "Your father made our yoke heavy; now therefore, lighten the burdensome service of your father, and his heavy yoke which he put on us and we will serve you" (1 Kings 12:4). In other words, if you keep taxing us out the wazoo, then we're going to walk. This demand was not unheard of at the time. It was a common practice among some nations that upon the installation of a new leader, certain previous oppressive governmental practices were halted.[14] This confrontation was Rehoboam's first test of his leadership, and the stakes couldn't have been higher. So, he told the people to go away and to come back in three days, when he would let them know his decision.

Taxed Enough Already

It has been witnessed throughout history that heavy taxation sets the stage for revolt and upheaval. When the burden of taxation reaches a tipping point, usually something bad happens. Take for instance our own history as a nation. The United States was birthed out of a rallying cry of "no taxation without representation."[15] The American colonists believed that for taxation to be fair, they

---

[14] J. A. Thompson, *The New American Commentary: 1, 2 Chronicle* (Nashville, TN: Broadman and Holman Publishers, 1994), 251.

[15] Historyofmassachusettes.org/American-revolution-acts/.

needed to have direct representation in the British Parliament in London. Otherwise, they felt the undue burden of supporting British military campaigns around the world. In spite of the colonists' complaints, the British Crown persisted in levying taxes contained in such impositions known as the Sugar, Currency, Stamp, Townshend, and Tea Acts. These coercive taxes levied against the colonists ignited the flame that led to the American Revolution. Thus, England's failure to address these grievances preceded "the shot heard around the world."[16] Like the American colonists, the citizens of the northern kingdom had endured enough of heavy taxation and injustice. They were ready for a change.

Bulletin Board Material

Rehoboam gave himself three days to make his decision. He sought advice from two groups of men. First, he called in his father's trusted advisors. These men had been around for a while. They told him to ease the tax burden on the people. "If you will be a servant to these people today, and serve them, and answer them, and speak good to them, then they will be your servants forever" (1 Kings 12:7). Next, he asked his friends, the guys with whom he grew up. Their advice was decidedly different. They said to tell the people, "My little finger shall be thicker than my father's waist. And now whereas my father put a heavy yoke on you, I will

---

[16] https://www.constitutionfacts.com/us-declaration-of-independence/the-shot-heard-round-the-world/.

add to your yoke; my father chastised you with whips, but I will chastise you with scourges" (1 Kings 12:10–11). Unfortunately, Rehoboam went with the advice of the younger guys, and as you can imagine, it went over like a lead balloon.

By listening to his friends instead of his father's advisors, Rehoboam created a public relations nightmare. His friend's nifty little saying became fodder for those who wanted to break away and form a new nation. In sports, these unfortunate statements made prior to a big game are known as "bulletin board material." Take for instance the unfortunate remark made by a Vanderbilt University football player following a surprising victory over then #18 ranked Kansas State. In his postgame exuberance, the player looked at the television camera and said, "Alabama, you're next."[17] Now if you know anything about college football, you know that was indeed a foolish statement. As expected, the Crimson Tide football team took the statement as a direct challenge. It was alpha male proving time. The following Saturday was a bloodbath, with Alabama winning 59–0. So, if you are in a tense situation that could turn on a dime, by all means don't say anything that could rally your opponent. Unfortunately, the words spoken by Rehoboam provided the rebels in the northern ten tribes with all the ammunition they needed to break off and form their own nation.

---

[17] https://www.seccountry.com/alabama/alabama-fans-relentlessly-troll-vandy-player-wanted-bama-59-0-beatdown.

Adjusting to the New Reality

Once the northern tribes followed through with their plans for secession, Rehoboam tried to act as though nothing had happened. He even sent out his chief tax collector to garner taxes from the north. This revenuer had unfortunately collected his last coin. He was brutally murdered, and Rehoboam had to abandon the north. However, once he arrived back in the south, he tried to muster up an army to quash the rebellion. A prophet warned him not to do so, and in spite of the people prodding him to go to war, Rehoboam wisely listened to the prophet. Scripture says, "So the king did not listen to the people: for the turn of events was from the LORD, that He might fulfill His word, which the LORD had spoken by Ahijah the Shilonite to Jeroboam the son of Nebat" (1 Kings 12:15). The turn of events was ordained by God, and no army on earth could stop it. Surprisingly, Rehoboam heeded the warning, and the breakaway was final.

Let's face it, Rehoboam had inherited a mess from his father. Even though he exercised bad judgment, the result was preordained by God. The kingdom had been split. Now, Rehoboam had to adjust to his new reality, and for the first three years, it looked promising. The southern kingdom, Judah, attracted those from the north, especially the Levites who were serious about worshipping the true God. This influx of devout believers had a stabilizing effect on Rehoboam's kingdom. Second Chronicles 11:17 says, "So they strengthened the kingdom of Judah and made Rehoboam the son of Solomon strong for three years because they walked in the way of David and Solomon for three years."

During this time, Rehoboam strengthened the kingdom and displayed a lot of wisdom with the decisions he made. It seemed as though he was going to be a wise king after all. However, as his situation improved, his commitment to God lessened. It has often been noted in life how one turns to God during the bad times, but the true test happens when the good times return.

Can You Handle Success?

In the early days of America, the Puritans left their mark in the New England colonies. Known for piety and hard work, they began to prosper. This prosperity led to some lessening of their piety. Famed Puritan pastor Cotton Mather shrewdly observed, "Religion brought forth prosperity and the daughter destroyed the mother."[18] Rehoboam was starting to feel good about himself. Second Chronicles 12:1 sums up his new attitude. "Now it came to pass when Rehoboam had established the kingdom and had strengthened himself that he forsook the law of the LORD and all Israel along with him." Amazing! It only took three years of improvement for his disloyal heart to reemerge.

One of my favorite athletes of all time is NFL Hall of Fame quarterback Kurt Warner. In the world of professional sports, he is the ultimate rags to riches story. Perhaps what I respect the most about Warner is that success did not destroy him. He was the same before and after he achieved superstar status. Not only did he stay faithful during the height of his NFL career, he also

---

[18] https://en.wikiquote.org/wiki/Cotton_Mather.

gracefully handled a downturn in which he had to play backup to two up-and-coming quarterbacks, Eli Manning with the Giants and Matt Leinart with the Cardinals. Despite his reduced role, he stayed focused and eventually led his second team to the Super Bowl. When Warner reflected on his incredible up-and-down journey, he said that he would like for people to remember him with these words: "Not the way I threw the football, not particular games that I won. But that they remember that here's a guy that believed, that worked hard, and—although things didn't always go in his favor—he continued to press through. And with his faith in himself and with his faith in God, he was able to accomplish great things."[19] Warner provides a wonderful example on how success affects people in different ways.

For Rehoboam, however, let's just say that success came with a big price tag. He pointed the nation full speed in the wrong direction. First Kings 14:22–24 gives details of this departure from the Lord. "Now Judah did evil in the sight of the Lord, and they provoked Him to jealousy with their sins which they committed, more than all that their fathers had done. For they also built for themselves high places, sacred pillars, and wooden images on every high hill and under every green tree. And there were also perverted persons in the land. They did according to all the abominations of the nations which the Lord had cast out before the children of Israel." Rehoboam did not have a loyal heart toward God. He was strictly a man of his circumstances.

---

[19] https://www.christianpost.com/news/kurt-warner-jesus-brought-me-here. html.

Go to Your Room

God could not let Rehoboam's transgression stand, so He raised up an instrument of His chastisement in the form of Shishak, king of Egypt. This Egyptian monarch invaded Judah and wreaked havoc on the southern kingdom. Eventually, even the sacred city of Jerusalem would experience his menacing presence as he and his men made off with Rehoboam's wealth. Of special note are the gold shields that the guards at the royal palace used. They seemed to have caught Shishak's eye, and he took them with him back to Egypt. Scripture notes how Rehoboam was quick to replace these ceremonial armaments with a lesser version made of bronze. The lesser value of the shields symbolized the "fading splendor" of the southern kingdom.[20] The nation's disobedience would not be blessed by God. This cycle of obedience and blessing followed by disobedience and punishment would become a hallmark of future kings. They just couldn't seem to keep a good thing going.

As Rehoboam passed off the scene, his life was summed up with these words in 2 Chronicles 12:14: "And he did evil, because he did not prepare his heart to seek the LORD." Wow! He was not ready for the big stage. He failed to prepare his heart, and both he and the nation suffered. How many people fail to prepare themselves for success? I'm not talking about skill. I'm talking about spiritual preparation. I'm talking about character and integrity. This lack of preparation shows up when the stakes

---

[20] Tony Merida, Exalting Jesus in *1 & 2 Kings, Christ-Centered Exposition* (Nashville, TN: B&H Publishing Group, 2015), 88.

are high. Unfortunately, those who are unprepared take a lot of people down with them.

Lesson to Learn

The biggest lesson we can learn from Rehoboam is the need to prepare ourselves for whatever the Lord wants us to do. Rehoboam was given the incredible privilege of being the king of Judah, but he had not prepared himself for the job. It's not that he didn't have previous warning that he was going to be king. It was common knowledge throughout the realm that he would be the next king. However, he squandered his opportunity, and the people of Judah suffered for his lack of preparation. For us, our preparation involves a combination of character and skill. Our character is shaped by a consistent walk with God. By reading and applying God's Word to our lives. By living with a dependence upon the Holy Spirit. By having a consistent accountability with others in our lives. Our skill is developed by doing our best with our God-given talent. By honing our craft. By working hard. By doing whatever we do with all our might as unto the Lord. Preparation makes us ready for those God-given opportunities that come our way.

Verses to Memorize

Psalm 1:1–3: "Blessed *is* the man who walks not in the counsel of the ungodly, nor stands in the path of sinners, nor sits in the seat of the scornful; but his delight *is* in the law of the Lord, and in His law he meditates day and night. He shall be like a tree planted by the rivers of water, that brings forth its fruit in its season, whose leaf also shall not wither; and whatever he does shall prosper."

Colossians 3:23–24: "And whatever you do, do it heartily, as to the Lord and not to men, knowing that from the Lord you will receive the reward of the inheritance; for you serve the Lord Christ."

Questions to Ponder

1. Rehoboam had an opportunity to bring healing to the nation. The northern tribes had grown weary under the heavy burden of overtaxation. Unfortunately, he listened to the incendiary advice his friends gave him instead of the wise counsel his father's trusted advisors gave him. Who do you go to for wise counsel? What qualifications do you look for in a counselor?

2. When everything went badly, Rehoboam got serious about his walk with God. However, when Rehoboam was able to strengthen himself and the southern kingdom began to prosper, he quickly turned away from the Lord. It seemed his commitment to God existed only when he was in trouble. Once the good times reappeared, Rehoboam no longer needed God. Can you walk closely with the Lord in both the good times and in the bad times? Does it take tragedy for you to walk closely with God? Can you handle prosperity and stay close to the Lord? How circumstantial is your faith?

3. In summing up the reign of Rehoboam, 2 Chronicles 12:14 says, "And he did evil because he did not prepare his heart to seek the LORD." Rehoboam was not spiritually ready for the opportunity that God gave him to become king. How are you preparing yourself for greater responsibility? Is your heart prepared to follow whatever path God may have for you to travel?

Chapter 2

Asa

Read 1 Kings 15:9–24 and 2 Chronicles 14–16.

We now skip to the reign of Asa, the fifth king of Judah in the lineage of David. Asa was the grandson of Rehoboam. His father, Abijam, was not a good man. Scripture says that Abijam "walked in all the sins of his father, which he had done before him; his heart was not loyal to the LORD his God, as was the heart of his father David" (1 Kings 15:3). Abijam occupied the throne but did not have a heart for God. As such, his reign was characterized by constant warfare with the northern kingdom. Even though Asa was in the line of David, he did not come out of a godly heritage. There was a consistent move away from God and toward idolatry. Asa was going to have to show himself to be different.

First One Hundred Days

Presidents in America are often judged by their first one hundred days in office. This standard of evaluation originated after the inauguration of Franklin D. Roosevelt. When Roosevelt became president in 1932, the nation was in distress. The economy was in a full depression. Unemployment was through the roof, and people needed someone to give them hope. So, during his first one hundred days, Roosevelt passed a whopping seventy-six new laws and laid the groundwork for what would become known as the New Deal.[21] He seized the moment and shaped the future. King Asa was also given such an opportunity, and he made the most of it.

What immediately stands out about Asa in 2 Chronicles 14 is that he was decisive in his actions. He immediately put his faith into practice with public policy. First, he handled the obvious. He removed the trappings of idolatry. If you are going to make changes, it is best to start at the top, and in Judaism, that begins with the first two commandments: "You shall have no other gods before me. You shall not make for yourself a carved image" (Exodus 20:3–4). For Asa to be true to God's Word, he would have to undo a lot of spiritual damage that his father inflicted upon the nation. This renovation would begin with the immediate removal of the idols that his father set up (1 Kings 15:12). Next, he told the people to seek and to obey God (2 Chronicles 14:4). Following these commands, he then began an extensive campaign to fortify

---

[21] https://www.cnn.com/2017/04/23/politics/donald-trump-history-100-days/index.html.

the cities of Judah. As a wise ruler, he saw himself as responsible for providing safety for the people under his rule.

Faith Is Meant to Be Tested

As is always the case, our faith will be challenged, and that was no different for King Asa. His challenge was in the form of Zerah the Ethiopian and his million-man army. Despite being outmanned two to one, Asa remained steadfast in his faith. Because he had nurtured and cultivated his walk with God, the natural thing for him to do was to approach this crisis with confidence in God instead of fear of the enemy. He prayed, "LORD, it is nothing for You to help, whether with many or with those who have no power; help us, O LORD our God, for we rest on You, and in Your name, we go against this multitude. O LORD, You are God, do not let man prevail against You" (2 Chronicles 14:11). Asa combined great faith with great courage, and God granted him a great victory. The Ethiopians were defeated, and the reforms of Asa were vindicated by God.

After the battle, Asa remained humble. His relationship with God seemed to really take off. A prophet named Azariah even gave him words of reassurance. The prophet told him, "The LORD is with you while you are with Him. If you seek Him, He will be found by you; but if you forsake Him, He will forsake you" (2 Chronicles 15:2). Wow! Talk about an incentive to maintain a close walk with God. But wait. There's more. He was also told, "Be strong and do not let your hands be weak, for your work shall be rewarded" (2 Chronicles 15:7). Stay close to God, and He will reward your efforts. Seems straightforward. Asa took these words to heart and continued to walk closely with God. He intensified his reforms, and the nation was definitely headed in the right direction. As a matter of fact, the change was so great that even some citizens of the northern kingdom began to make their way south. The blessing of God was evident for all to see.

Taking Care of Unfinished Business

In the fifteenth year of his reign, Asa convened a large gathering in order to recommit the nation to seek God with all their heart and soul. This commitment was a big deal. As part of Asa's commitment to God, he removed his grandmother, Maachah, from being queen mother. Her removal was in response to an obscene image she had erected in honor of the Canaanite goddess Asherah (2 Chronicles 15:16). Let's face it. When you're serious enough to remove your own grandmother from the palace because of her idolatry, you're in it for real.

For the next twenty years, there was peace in the kingdom. Up to this point, Asa had met every challenge with unquestionable trust in God. He had passed the test, and he had exercised fantastic spiritual leadership both publicly and privately. He had destroyed the idolatrous practices his father left, and he had removed his wayward grandmother from her kingdom position. However, as the next two decades unfolded, Asa appeared to become dull in his walk with God. This spiritually weakened position was about to reveal itself.

You Can't Live off Yesterday's Bread

You can't live off yesterday's victories. It's like Americans basing their sense of security on the fact the Allies defeated Germany and Japan in WWII. There are always challenges that require vigilance on our part. Judah had experienced twenty years of peace. However, Baasha, the king of Israel, suddenly shattered this serene atmosphere. In a provocative move, he constructed a fort five miles north of Jerusalem. This military base was on the major north-south trade route. If left unchallenged, Judah would suffer both economically and militarily. King Baasha was emboldened by his nonaggression treaty with King Ben-Hadad of Syria. Asa feared a dual alliance between these two kingdoms would be disastrous, so he secretly bribed Ben-Hadad to betray his alliance with Israel.[22] This payoff was not cheap. As one commentator noted, "it cost Asa the contents of the temple treasury, some personal wealth, his integrity, and his standing with God."[23] Once Baasha saw that the Syrian king had betrayed him, he withdrew, and a major crisis was avoided. On the surface, it appeared that Asa's secret diplomacy was a rousing success. However, there was a big problem. In all his planning, Asa did not consult God. His plans were birthed out of fear instead of faith. Being pragmatic is not always bad. However, when it is based on fear instead of faith, it can cause more problems than it solves. In

---

[22] J. A. Thompson, p. 274.

[23] Winfried Corduan, *I & II Chronicles, Holman Old Testament Commentary* (Nashville, TN: Broadman and Holman Publishers, 2004), p. 259.

Asa's case, it was the decision that led to a downward spiral in his walk with God.

Because Asa did not seek God's wisdom, God sent a prophet with these words of rebuke for the king:

> Because you have relied on the king of Syria and have not relied on the LORD your God, therefore the army of the king of Syria has escaped from our hand. Were not the Ethiopians and the Lubim not a huge army with very many chariots and horsemen? Yet, because you relied on the LORD, He delivered them into your hand. For the eyes of the LORD run to and fro throughout the whole earth, to show Himself strong on behalf of those whose heart is loyal to Him. In this you have done foolishly; therefore, from now on you shall have wars. (2 Chronicles 16:7–9)

In the process of solving a short-term problem, Asa created a much larger long-term one.

The End Doesn't Always Justify the Means

Admittedly, the words from the prophet were hard for this long-reigning monarch to take. He had just avoided a major confrontation with the northern kingdom. There was peace. His plan worked. However, it did not have God's approval. The diplomacy was pragmatic, but it was not of God. His plan did not address the root problem. God's plan would have brought a more lasting peace. Unfortunately, now there would be war. Even though his shrewd decision temporarily brought peace, the end does not justify the means. God would have defeated both foes, and no one would have had to be paid off. Just because an action brings about a desired result does not mean it is right. It may very well result in a forfeiture of future blessings.

Even Fonzie Isn't Always Right

When I was growing up, one of the most popular shows on TV was *Happy Days*. The most memorable character was a leather-jacket-wearing hoodlum named Fonzie. He was the epitome of cool, as evidenced by his trademark expression "Aaaaay!" However, one rule of thumb was that Fonzie was always right. He was never wrong. On several episodes, he struggled to mouth the words, "I was wrong." Well, King Asa could identify with Fonzie. He could not say he was wrong. Instead of repenting for his unauthorized diplomacy, he responded with bitterness and defiance. These attitudes were very uncharacteristic for someone with his track record. However, he was so enraged that he became the first king to persecute a prophet. He put the seer in jail and oppressed some of his own people. He was bitter toward God. Unfortunately, Asa would not admit he was wrong and never got over it.

Asa's defiant disposition lasted for three years until he contracted an unspecified disease in his feet. His condition was said to be severe, but even in his sickness, scripture says, "He did not seek the LORD but the physicians" (2 Chronicles 16:12).

Within two years, he was dead. After forty-one years on the throne, he was buried with his fathers. Asa did not finish well. He did wrong and never got over it.

How many people have gone to their grave never admitting that something they did was wrong? A relationship was never restored because they would not admit fault. A decision could not be made right because they would not admit they were wrong. The bitterness poisoned their soul, and they died a very unhappy death.

Lesson to Learn

The biggest lesson we can learn from Asa is that we need to admit when we are wrong. Asa got too confident in his own abilities apart from his dependence upon God. He made a shrewd move to bribe the Syrian king, but his actions were not authorized by God. When he was confronted by one of God's prophets, he chose defiance. Asa would not listen to the prophet. In his bitterness, he decided not to seek God anymore in his life. Even as he faced a terminal illness, he sought the physicians but not God. His lack of contrition led to bitterness toward God. We must not be like Asa. We must be able to admit our failures. We must be ready to respond in a positive manner when we are convicted by God's Word over some issue in our life. We are never above correction. We must maintain a teachable spirit and a willingness to change.

Verses to Memorize

Proverbs 28:13: "He who covers his sins will not prosper, but whoever confesses and forsakes them will have mercy."

First John 1:9: "If we confess our sins, He is faithful and just to forgive us and to cleanse us from all unrighteousness."

Questions

1. Asa had to make some very difficult decisions concerning family. He had to undo the works of his father, and he had to remove his own grandmother from her royal position. He had to break away from the sinful foundation that his family had laid for him. He had to choose his faith over his family. Do you find it hard to break out of old, sinful family habits? Is it hard to admit to the sinfulness of previous generations? Do you put family members ahead of your faith?

2. Asa engaged in secret diplomacy with the king of Syria, and it worked. The only problem was that he did not consult God. He was pragmatic, but he did not seek God first. Have you ever made a choice that seemed the right thing to do but you did not seek God first? Are pragmatism and faith always opposed to each other? How do you know which one to choose?

3. When the prophet confronted Asa, he chose rebellion over repentance. Asa could not admit he was wrong. His alliance with Ben-Hadad brought short-term peace but forfeited long-term blessings. He would not admit he was wrong, and he let his bitterness poison the rest of his life. Is there a relationship that you can restore if you admit your faults? Do you have a hard time admitting when you are wrong? Do you have any bitterness toward God or toward another individual? What can you do to make things right?

Chapter 3

Jehoshaphat

Read 1 Kings 22:41–50 and 2 Chronicles 17–20.

Jehoshaphat came to the throne when he was thirty-five years old, and he reigned for twenty-five years. For the first three years of his reign, he had a coregency with his father, and then for twenty-two years he reigned alone. His father, Asa, did a lot of positive things for the kingdom, and overall, he was considered a good king. However, in the last several years of his life, he did not seek God. He had been rebuked by a prophet, and he responded by putting this man of God in a dungeon. Additionally, he persecuted the citizens of his kingdom, and in general, he took on an adversarial tone. The last three years of his life were spent in anguish as he suffered a disease in his feet. What's sad is that in his illness he did not seek God. Instead, he sought the help of physicians to the exclusion of God. Jehoshaphat witnessed these unfortunate events firsthand. He saw his father leave this world with a bitter soul toward God.

Scripture tells us that Jehoshaphat was a good king. "Now the LORD was with Jehoshaphat, because he walked in the ways of his father David. And he took delight in the ways of the LORD" (2 Chronicles 17:3, 6). He even sent the priests throughout the land to teach the people the Word of God. As his power and wealth increased, even some of his enemies brought him presents of appeasement (2 Chronicles 17:11). However, in 2 Chronicles 18, we see the beginning of his penchant for making terrible alliances.

Arranged Marriage Gone Bad

It has long been a custom for monarchs to marry off their children for the purpose of achieving national security. Although this practice has had some success, there have also been some colossal failures. Take for instance the late sixteenth-century marriage of Henri de Bourbon to Marguerite de Valois. This arranged marriage was for the purpose of uniting two feuding royal French families during the height of the Wars of Religion.[24] This attempt at nuptial diplomacy resulted in the infamous Saint Bartholomew's Day Massacre in which an estimated seventy thousand French protestants were murdered by Catholics.[25] This well-intentioned but misguided attempt for peace closely resembles Jehoshaphat's failed efforts.

Jehoshaphat allied himself with the wicked king Ahab. Ahab was the king of the northern kingdom. Previously, the northern

---

[24] https://www.history.com/news/royal-weddings-gone-bad.

[25] https://www.britannica.com/event/Massacre-of-Saint-Bartholomews-Day.

kingdom and Judah had been at war. Jehoshaphat had initially strengthened himself militarily against the north, but for some reason he decided to go in a different direction. As a way of securing his northern border, Jehoshaphat used the age-old method of diplomacy through matrimony. In other words, he married off his son to the daughter of Ahab and his treacherous wife, Jezebel. Talk about a bad move. Oftentimes when someone uses worldly thinking in order to provide security, it does not end well.

Remember, the northern kingdom had decided from its origin to engage in idolatry. Jeroboam, the first king of the northern kingdom, devised a way to prevent his people from wanting to return to Jerusalem to worship. He made two golden calves and set them up in Dan and Bethel for people to worship. In direct defiance of scripture, he made priests out of every tribe and not just Levi. He even changed the calendar feast days to minimize the commonality between the north and the south. Jeroboam's family was eventually deposed by a military coup led by a man named Omri. Omri was succeeded by his son, Ahab, who married a pagan princess named Jezebel.

Ahab and Jezebel were one of the most diabolical couples in human history. Just look at how the Bible describes this dastardly duo. "But there was no one like Ahab who sold himself to do wickedness in the sight of the LORD, because Jezebel his wife stirred him up" (1 Kings 21:25). These are not the type of people you want for your in-laws. So, why did Jehoshaphat set up his son with their daughter? Because it seemed like the logical thing to do. However, this marital alliance was not necessary, and it had deadly ramifications for Jehoshaphat's family.

Family connections were not the only unholy alliance that Jehoshaphat made with Ahab. A few years after the nuptials, Jehoshaphat went to the north to visit with the in-laws. When he arrived, King Ahab prepared a huge feast for Jehoshaphat and his entourage. However, there was a purpose for this hospitality. Ahab wanted Jehoshaphat to join him in a military alliance against the Syrian-controlled city of Ramoth Gilead. Immediately, Jehoshaphat gave his support for the joint venture, with one caveat. They needed to seek God's will on the matter first. Now, Jehoshaphat should not have had to consult God on such matters. The northern kingdom was apostate. God would not be in any type of alliance between the two kingdoms. However, Jehoshaphat was invested in the family of Ahab and Jezebel. His son was married to their daughter. They were going to share grandbabies. So, he advised Ahab that they should seek the will of God.

Ahab's version of seeking the will of God was to call in four hundred false prophets. These members of the clergy were nothing more than a bunch of yes-men. When Ahab asked them if they should go to war, they responded with good news. "Go up for God will deliver it into the king's hand" (2 Chronicles 18:5). Immediately, Jehoshaphat recognized the false words spoken by the prophets, so he asked Ahab if there was a true prophet of God to be found. There was one, but Ahab hated him because "he never prophesizes good for me, but always evil" (2 Chronicles 18:7).

The prophet's name was Michaiah. Before he was ushered

into the presence of the two monarchs, he was coached as to how he should answer. The king's messenger told the prophet, "Now listen the words of the prophets with one accord encourage the king. Therefore, please let your word be like the word of one of them and speak encouragement" (2 Chronicles 18:12). In other words, forget about God's will. The main thing is that the king feels good about what you say. So, when Michaiah went before the king, he told him a bunch of fluff. He said, "Go and prosper, and they shall be delivered into your hand" (2 Chronicles 18:14). Immediately, Ahab knew the prophet was just saying what the king wanted to hear, so he put him under an oath to tell him the truth. When placed under such oath, the prophet let Ahab have it with both barrels. The prophet said Ahab would go to battle and would die. End of story. For his insolence before the king, Michaiah was struck by one of the false prophets and mocked. Ahab then responded by throwing the prophet into prison with the promise that he would kill him when he returned from battle.

As Ahab and Jehoshaphat prepared to go to battle, it became apparent that Ahab was a little unhinged by what the prophet said. On paper, the Syrian-controlled city of Ramoth Gilead should have been no match for their dual alliance. However, the words spoken by the prophet were ominous, and Ahab was rattled. So, in a classic move, Ahab convinced Jehoshaphat to wear his kingly robes, while he would dress as a common soldier. Perhaps, in Ahab's mind, he thought he could beat the prophecy by disguising himself and that disaster would come upon the kingly dressed Jehoshaphat instead. Like a dupe, Jehoshaphat went along with the scheme. When the battle got intense, all of the Syrian forces made a beeline toward Jehoshaphat, thinking that he was Ahab. When Jehoshaphat saw his dire situation, he cried out to God, and God delivered him. Meanwhile, as Ahab masqueraded as a common soldier, an arrow was randomly shot by an enemy combatant, and it just so happened to strike the king between the joints of his armor. It was a fatal wound, and Ahab died.

When Jehoshaphat returned home from his near-death experience, a prophet confronted him with these stunning words: "Should you help the wicked and love those who hate the LORD" (2 Chronicles 19:2). For the second time, Jehoshaphat had intertwined his kingdom with that of the ungodly Ahab and Jezebel. He had united the two families through marriage and had entered into a military alliance. Both times without God's approval and both times with disastrous consequences. Why would Jehoshaphat ally himself with a family who was known for their gross idolatry? Jezebel had even persecuted the prophets of God (1 Kings 18:4). Yet Jehoshaphat would join his family to theirs. Talk about a serious lapse of judgment. However, after his debacle in the north, Jehoshaphat recommitted himself and led the people back to a greater dependence upon the Lord. He even told his officials, "You shall act in the fear of the Lord, faithfully and with a loyal heart" (1 Chronicles 19:9).

Jehoshaphat needed to be close to God because he would soon face an invasion by an alliance of nations. The odds were so grim that Jehoshaphat was afraid. However, this fear led him to seek God's protection. He instructed the people to fast, and he prayed an incredibly powerful prayer that ended with these words: "For we have no power against this great multitude that is coming against us; nor do we know what to do, but our eyes are upon You" (2 Chronicles 20:12). What a great prayer of dependence. We don't know what to do, but we are looking to You. In response to this prayer, God sent word through a prophet to assure Jehoshaphat of victory. The prophet said, "Listen, all you of Judah and you inhabitants of Jerusalem, and you, King Jehoshaphat! Thus says the LORD to you; 'Do not be afraid nor dismayed because of this great multitude, for the battle is not yours, but God's'" (2 Chronicles 20:14). Buoyed by these words, Jehoshaphat led his army into the wilderness of Tekoa for battle. As the time of conflict approached, God turned the three invading armies on one another, and they destroyed themselves. When the army of Judah approached the scene, the carnage of the enemy was everywhere. Judah had been saved without having to fight. With the invading alliance defeated, Judah was able to collect an abundance of loot. Not only was the nation saved militarily, but they prospered economically as well.

Unequally Yoked

It is always interesting to read about the biggest mistakes in history, especially as they relate to money. Some blunders are hilarious, while others will break your heart. Some, however, are just flat-out ridiculous. Take for instance the case of the lost space orbiter. In 1999, NASA lost a $125 million spacecraft because, in programming the orbiter, they used the metric system, while the contractor, Lockheed Martin, used the English system of measurement. This discrepancy prevented the lab on earth from communicating with the orbiter in outer space, thus making navigation impossible.[26] The two systems of measurement cannot be used simultaneously. One must be chosen over the other. Otherwise, it just won't work. The same could be said of Jehoshaphat. He kept trying to have fellowship with the darkness of the northern kingdom. However, it just would not work.

The Futility Continues

Despite this great victory, Jehoshaphat was not through with his ungodly alliance with the northern kingdom. Despite his previous misadventures, he made one last overture to the north. He entered into a joint business venture with King Ahab's son, Ahaziah. Together, they built a fleet of ships for trade purposes. However, God destroyed the ships with a storm and sent a prophet with these words: "Because you have allied yourself with Ahaziah, the Lord has destroyed your works" (2 Chronicles 20:37). After the fleet was destroyed, Ahaziah tried to get Jehoshaphat to once again enter the shipping business with him, but this time Jehoshaphat declined the offer.

In the final analysis, Jehoshaphat is listed as a good king. However, he had one besetting issue. He kept making alliances with the ungodly family of Ahab and Jezebel. This arranged

---

[26] http://www.businessinsider.com/worst-mistakes-in-history-2011-4#nasa-uses-the-metric-system-while-lockheed-martin-uses-the-english-system-when-building-a-satellite-4.

marriage between his son and Ahab's daughter would bring death and destruction into his family. His military alliance with Ahab almost got him killed in battle. And his business enterprise with this wicked family ended in financial loss. God was not going to let Jehoshaphat connect himself with Ahab and Jezebel and prosper.

Stuck on Bad Choices

One of the greatest natural disasters to ever hit the United States was Hurricane Katrina. This devastating storm destroyed a major city and ruined many political careers. The storm simply exposed the weak leadership and corruption of the city of New Orleans. It also highlighted the ineptitude of a bloated bureaucracy in responding to human need. In the midst of all of this political and bureaucratic disappointment, one man rose above all others. His name was Lieutenant General Russell Honore. This three-star general was sent to oversee and streamline the recovery of New Orleans. His no-nonsense style led New Orleans' Mayor Ray Nagin to refer to him as "that John Wayne dude."[27] During one of his most contentious press conferences, Honoree tried to point the reporters forward to another impending storm named Rita that was barreling down on New Orleans. Instead of dealing with the current threat, the stubborn reporters kept wanting to ask questions about what went wrong with Katrina. Finally, an exasperated Honore simply told the reporters that they needed to

[27] http://www.cnn.com/2005/US/09/02/honore.profile/.

quit getting stuck on the wrong way of thinking.[28] They needed to move forward and deal with the current crisis. However, they did not want to deal with the present. In their stubbornness, the reporters were stuck in the past. When it came to the family of Ahab, it is safe to say that Jehoshaphat got stuck on unwise thinking. For years, Jehoshaphat thought that he could incur God's blessings as he made alliances with his wicked counterparts from the north. At great expense, he learned that he was wrong. Unfortunately, his obsession with this wicked family would come back to haunt his own family long after his death.

The Aftermath

When Jehoshaphat died, he left the throne to his son Jehoram. This was a poor choice for a successor. It seems that Jehoram was more influenced by his ungodly wife, Athalia, than he was by his righteous father, Jehoshaphat. Scripture says that Jehoram "walked in the way of the kings of Israel, just as the house of Ahab had done, for he had the daughter of Ahab as a wife; and he did evil in the sight of the LORD" (2 Chronicles 21:6). Part of this evil involved killing off all his brothers once he had established himself as king. This fratricide decimated the lineage of the Davidic dynasty, but it satisfied the desire of his bloodthirsty wife. The woman that his father, Jehoshaphat, gave to him to bring security instead brought death.

---

[28] https://www.npr.org/2015/08/27/434385285/swept-up-in-the-storm-hurricane-katrinas-key-players-then-and-now.

Jehoram's reign was not blessed by God. As a matter of fact, God worked against him. During Jehoram's reign, God stirred up the Edomites, Philistines, and Arabians. God even sent the prophet Elijah to Jehoram with a letter of rebuke that ended with these ominous words: "You will become very sick with a disease of your intestines, until your intestines come out by reason of the sickness, day by day" (2 Chronicles 21:15). Jehoram was going to experience more than an upset tummy. He was going to experience a long, grueling demise. After two years of suffering, his intestines came out of him, and he died in severe pain. At his death, no one was moved. Scripture says that they didn't burn the ceremonial spices for him, nor did they bury him in the tomb of the kings. His funeral was appropriate for a detestable man.

After Jehoram's death, the people made his youngest son, Ahaziah, king. Unfortunately, Ahaziah was just another chip off the old block. He was a despicable man who was under the same ungodly influence as his father. His mother, Athalia, continued to steer the nation in an ungodly direction. These weak kings were no match for this ungodly spawn of Jezebel. Scripture says that Ahaziah "walked in the ways of the house of Ahab, for his mother advised him to do wickedly" (2 Chronicles 22:3). With Athalia guiding him, Ahaziah entered a closer relationship with the northern kingdom. After all, they were family. However, this familial connection would be his downfall. When the house of Ahab fell to the forces of Jehu, Ahaziah happened to be in the wrong place at the wrong time, and he died at the hands of Jehu. So, Ahaziah's brief reign came to a sudden end.

Because there was not an immediate heir, the ungodly Athalia grabbed the throne for herself. She then did her customary practice and ordered the execution of all the other potential royal heirs. Now, the throne was hers alone. Fortunately, one young royal heir was kept alive. His name was Joash, and this baby boy would eventually be her undoing.

Athalia is part of the legacy of Jehoshaphat. He was responsible for bringing this ungodly woman into the family. She was meant to bring security and peace. However, good intentions don't make up for nonbiblical actions.

Lesson to Learn

The biggest lesson we can learn from Jehoshaphat is not to make close alliances with those who do not share our faith. Even though Jehoshaphat was a righteous king, he continued to make partnerships with the wicked Ahab and Jezebel. He joined them through a marriage, a military campaign, and a business venture. Each partnership ended with disaster. In the New Testament, Christians are warned, "Do not be unequally yoked together with unbelievers. For what fellowship has righteousness with lawlessness? And what communion has light with darkness?" (2 Corinthians 6:14). Believers are admonished to not enter into any type of relationship that would "lead to a compromise of Christian standards or jeopardize consistency of Christian witness."[29] When

---

[29] W. Harold Mare and Murray J. Harris, *The Expositor's Bible Commentary: 1 & 2 Corinthians*, (Grand Rapids, MI: Zondervan Publishing House, 1995), 187.

there are two competing worldviews involved in a partnership, someone will eventually have to change. Believers should not put themselves in such a position.

Verses to Memorize

Second Corinthians 6:14: "Do not be unequally yoked together with unbelievers. For what fellowship has righteousness with lawlessness? And what communion has light with darkness?"

Matthew 6:24: "No one can serve two masters; for either he will hate the one and love the other, or else he will be loyal to the one and despise the other. You cannot serve God and mammon."

Questions to Ponder

1. Scripture says that believers are not to be unequally yoked with unbelievers and that light has no fellowship with darkness. Despite his otherwise righteous character, Jehoshaphat kept joining with the ungodly family of Ahab and Jezebel. Why do you think the Bible warns against such an alliance? Are you involved in any alliance that taints your testimony and dulls your conscience?

2. Jehoshaphat continued to make the same mistake. He entered into a family, military, and business partnership with the family of Ahab and Jezebel. He was stuck on making the same

bad choices. Do you continue to make the same bad choices? How can you break out of such a destructive pattern?

3. Unfortunately, our bad decisions don't die when we do. After his death, Jehoshaphat's family was decimated by his wicked daughter-in-law. By marrying off his son for security purposes, he brought death and destruction into his family. Are there any decisions you are currently making that will be hard for your family to deal with when you die? What kind of a legacy are you leaving?

Chapter 4

Joash

Read 2 Kings 11–12 and 2 Chronicles 22–24.

A Ruined Legacy

At one time baseball was without a doubt America's favorite pastime. The pennant races brought excitement to the long summer days, and baseball players were household names. But something happened that tarnished baseball's reputation. The culprit came in the form of performance enhancing drugs better known as human growth hormones and anabolic steroids. Star players such as Barry Bonds, Mark McGuire and Sammy Sosa cheated in order to break records. Suddenly, heroes became zeroes. Instead of speeches at the Hall of Fame there were testimonies before congressional committees and grand juries. The excitement of the race to break the records of baseball fixtures such as Roger Maris and Hank Aaron was replaced with disappointment and shame. It must be noted that poor decisions ruin a legacy.

The same can be said of Jehoshaphat. His legacy was ruined by the brutal actions of his daughter in law Athalia. This offspring of Ahab and Jezebel managed to murder all the heirs of Ahaziah except one, an infant boy named Joash. This child was hidden away by his aunt Jehoshabeath, the sister of Ahaziah. Jehoshabeath was married to the priest Jehoiada. Wisely, she used this connection with the temple in order to secure a safe hiding place for Joash, who was the only remaining heir to the Davidic throne. This development was big stuff. God had said that the Messiah would come through the lineage of David, and almost all his heirs were wiped out. It makes one realize the satanic control that was exerted upon Ahab's ungodly family. Fortunately, Joash could not be in better hands. His uncle Jehoiada was a godly man who did what it took to ensure that Joash continued the Davidic dynasty.

The Coup Better Work

There are many famous coups in history. Men such as Napoleon Bonaparte, Francisco Franco, Idi Amin, and Augusto Pinochet came to power as a result of a coup. Classically defined, a coup is "A quick and decisive seizure of governmental power by a strong military or political group. In contrast to a revolution a coup does not involve a mass uprising."[30] Therefore, a coup must have extremely good planning and precise timing. When a coup goes badly, it usually ends in death for the conspirators. Take for

---

[30] http://www.dictionary.com/browse/coup-d-etat.

instance the attempted coup to take out Adolph Hitler in 1944. Code named Valkyrie by its participants, the coup involved an assassination attempt on Hitler at his secret command post in East Prussia called the Wolf's Lair.[31] During a meeting on July 20, 1944, Lieutenant Colonel Claus Schenk von Stauffenberg had a time bomb in his briefcase set to go off at 12:42 p.m. Before the bomb went off, von Stauffenberg dismissed himself from the meeting to take a call. The briefcase was left under the table near Hitler. Unfortunately, another officer moved the briefcase farther down the table away from Hitler. When the bomb went off, four people died, but Hitler escaped with minor injuries.[32] Afterward, there was confusion as to whether Hitler was dead, and this lack of clarity made the conspirators indecisive. This lapse of action proved to be fatal. Von Stauffenberg and approximately two hundred coconspirators were rounded up and executed. The lack of decisiveness and bad timing doomed the coup attempt. The coup attempted in Judah involved a priest and a seven-year-old boy. There was no room for error.

Strategic Plan for a Preferred Future

Everything hinged upon Athalia being removed from the throne and Joash being installed to his rightful place. However, Joash was an infant who was incapable of claiming the throne for himself, so he was hidden in the temple away from the knowledge

---

[31] https://www.history.com/topics/july-plot.

[32] https://www.britannica.com/event/July-Plot.

of his evil grandmother, Athalia. In the seventh year of Joash's life, Jehoiada made an incredibly bold move. He orchestrated a coup to take out this evil usurper. The stakes were literally life or death, so he had to be strategic and stealth. Fortunately for Jehoiada, nobody liked Athalia.

The first move that Jehoiada made was to enter into a covenant with the five captains of the temple guard. Once this alliance was established, these key military leaders fanned out across the nation to inform the Levites and their family heads about the planned coup. These leaders met up in Jerusalem and covenanted together inside the temple. So, the military and the religious leaders were all on board. The coup was to take place during the changing of the guard at the temple. This timing would allow a large group of soldiers to gather without undue notice. All these soldiers would be armed with the military equipment left in the temple by King David. Once the crucial moment arrived, seven-year-old Joash would be hastily ushered into the temple, surrounded by armed guards on all sides. Once the crown was placed on his head and he was anointed king by the priest, everyone would shout, "Long live the king." When the time came, the plan was executed perfectly, down to the last detail.

Meanwhile, Grandma Athalia was relaxing in the palace. It seemed like everyone got the text about a new king except her. All of Jerusalem was running toward the temple. This was a big-time development. Athalia ran to the temple, and when she saw the newly crowned boy king, she tore her clothes and cried, "Treason! Treason!" Kind of ironic that a conniving, murderous woman such as Athalia would have the audacity to call someone else treasonous. Long story short, Jehoiada didn't want to make a mess in the temple, so he had the guards escort Athalia out of the temple, and she was executed in the palace. The people also went and tore down the temple of Baal and killed the pagan high priest. The Davidic dynasty was restored, thanks to the exploits of the husband-wife team of Jehoiada and Jehoshabeath.

Jehoiada was a man with nerves of steel. His coup was a bold move preceded by precise planning. Jehoiada carefully coordinated the support of the military and religious leaders of the nation in order to crown Joash as king. He was playing with high stakes, so he had to be precise, and fortunately for the nation, he was up to the job. Jehoiada closed the deal by making a covenant between himself, the people, and the new seven-year-old king. Under this agreement, Jehoiada would serve as King Joash's advisor. And truth be told, Joash could not have been in better hands. Jehoiada was a man of the Book. He carefully followed the words of scripture as he advised the king.

So long as Jehoiada was his counselor, Joash was a good king. Scripture says, "Joash did what was right in the sight of the LORD all the days of Jehoiada the priest" (2 Chronicles 24:2). As Joash grew under the tutelage of Jehoiada, he developed a love for the temple. This is understandable since the temple was his secret hideout for the first seven years of his life. So, it is no surprise that Joash wanted to improve and refurbish the hallowed place. Under the rule of Athalia, the temple had been looted and otherwise neglected. Now, Joash was going to make sure that it got the attention it deserved. The temple was now over one hundred years old, and it was due for a facelift. However, Joash made the decisions about raising funds for the temple restoration all by himself. He did not seek Jehoiada's counsel. This unilateral decision-making was not good, and the results were anemic.

Joash's plans for a revenue stream for the temple repairs were horribly flawed. He had commissioned the Levites to collect the money from the various offerings that the people gave. However, this money was already allocated for temple maintenance and support of the priests.[33] It's like wanting to build a new school and then getting the money for the project out of the teachers' salaries. No one wouldn't expect the teachers to be too excited about collecting the money out of their own pockets. Scripture says that the priests did not do it quickly. As a matter of fact, the money came in so slowly that Joash summoned the high priest and asked him what was going on. Jehoiada explained the situation, and another solution was proposed. A box would be placed at the temple to receive voluntary contributions from the people. The money stream would be from contributions and not from taxes. And the people responded overwhelmingly. The collection was so successful that the temple was restored and reinforced, and the excess money was used to make the temple utensils. This project was a great boost for a nation that needed a few good breaks.

---

[33] Warren Wiersbe. *Be Distinct* (David C. Cook Publishing Colorado Springs, CO: 2002), 117.

When You Lose Your Best Counselor

Boxing great Mike Tyson is an interesting case. It is said that by the time he was thirteen years old, he had been arrested thirty-eight times.[34] Fortunately, he was taken by his detention counselor to a local gym, where he was introduced to Cus D'Amato, a local boxing manager.[35] D'Amato immediately recognized Tyson's potential and eventually adopted him as his son. In just three years, Tyson became a junior Olympic gold medalist. His star was rising faster than anyone's in professional boxing history. Unfortunately, D'Amato passed away on November 4, 1985, a date that one sports writer refers to as the day that boxing died.[36] After D'Amato's death, Tyson's life would devolve into a cesspool of immoral and dangerous behavior. His new advisor, Don King, had an adverse effect upon Tyson's behavior. The restraints were gone, and caution was thrown to the wind. According to legal proceedings, Tyson eventually accused King of bilking him out of tens of millions of dollars.[37] It goes to show that a young man needs the help of an older, trusted counselor, especially when he has a lot of power and influence. Like Tyson, Joash needed a wise counselor and guide, and he had one so long as Jehoiada lived.

---

[34] https://www.nytimes.com/2003/06/01/sports/sports-of-the-times-mike-tyson-should-stop-all-his-vile-talking-and-just-fight.html.

[35] http://bleacherreport.com/articles/218074-mike-tyson-and-the-day-that-boxing-died.

[36] http://bleacherreport.com/articles/218074-mike-tyson-and-the-day-that-boxing-died.

[37] http://www.nydailynews.com/archives/news/tyson-ko-don-king-article-1.792439.

Bad Counselors Give Bad Advice

When Jehoiada died at the age of 130, Joash became a different man. Unfortunately, this change was not for the better. Here is how scripture describes the metamorphosis that took place in Joash's life after the death of Jehoiada: "Now after the death of Jehoiada the leaders of Judah came and bowed down to the king, and the king listened to them. Therefore, they left the house of the Lord God of their fathers and served wooden images and idols" (2 Chronicles 24:17–18).

Joash's new advisors led him away from God and back into idolatry. It seems that Joash's faith was only as strong as the chief influencers in his life. In His faithfulness, God sent prophets to bring the people back to Himself, but they refused. Finally, Jehoiada's son, Zechariah, confronted the king with a message from the Lord. He said, "Why do you transgress the commandments of the Lord, so that you cannot prosper? Because you have forsaken the Lord, He has forsaken you" (2 Chronicles 24:20). These words only served the purpose of making Joash and his new advisors angry, so with the king's consent, an angry mob stoned the prophet to death. Joash killed the son of the couple who had saved his own life as a baby. The line had been crossed, and correction was on its way in the form of a foreign army.

Undoing Your Life's Work

There are some people who accomplish great things in life but who do not finish well. Others are able to tear down in a moment what it took years to build. Take Gerald Ratner for instance. At one time, he was the CEO of one of the largest jewelry chains in the world. Headquartered in the United Kingdom, his stores spread out across the Atlantic into America. He was a very successful man who enjoyed the lifestyle of the rich and famous. That was until he made a fateful speech to the Institute of Directors on April 23, 1991. Thousands of celebrities, business leaders, and journalists attended the event. During his speech, Ratner stunned the crowd when he said that the reason his company could sell a particular piece of jewelry at such a discounted price and still make a profit was because the product was basically a piece of junk.[38] After this unfortunate comment, Ratner had even more to say. He said that the price that his company sold a pair of earrings for was "cheaper than a shrimp sandwich from Marks and Spencer, but probably would not last as long."[39] His comments caused the value of his company to go into a free fall. So extensive was the damage that Ratner was removed from his position, and the company had to rename itself in order to survive. Like Ratner, Joash undid his life's work. The very temple that he had restored was pawned off in a futile attempt to avoid a foreign invasion. It seems that it doesn't take much to undo your life's work.

---

[38] https://www.telegraph.co.uk/business/2017/08/03/mirren-nine-times-people-undermined-products-supposed-selling/.

[39] https://www.businessblogshub.com/2012/09/the-man-who-destroyed-his-multi-million-dollar-company-in-10-seconds/.

Crash and Burn

Joash committed a grievous sin. He followed the counsel of his wicked advisors, and now it was time to pay the price. In the spring of that year, the Syrian army showed up on a winning note, having run roughshod over the Philistines in Gath. Despite the Syrian's inferior numbers, Joash was scared. He had left his faith and run headlong into idolatry. Now, at this crucial moment, he turned to bribery instead of the Lord. In his fallen condition, Joash emptied the temple of its contents and gave these riches to the Syrian king Hazael, hoping to pay his way out of the confrontation. However, a battle ensued, and Joash was severely wounded. The victorious Syrian king took an enormous amount of wealth out of Jerusalem and left an injured Joash in his wake. While Joash was recovering from his wounds, two of his own servants assassinated him. His death was payback for what he did to the prophet Zachariah. At his death, the people chose not to bury him in the tomb of the kings. His life was not considered worthy of such an honor.

Lesson to Learn

Joash tended to take on the nature of his closest advisors. He was a chameleon. When the righteous Jehoiada was alive, Joash lived a righteous lifestyle. Once Jehoiada died, Joash took on the nature of his new unrighteous advisors. He even consented to the death of a prophet. Because he lacked an anchor for his faith, Joash wound up undoing the good that he had previously done for the temple. It is very important that we choose carefully those from whom we take advice. Our faith should shape our relationships instead of our relationships shaping our faith. Joash's faith was shaped by those who were closest to him. This arrangement was a recipe for disaster.

Verses to Memorize

First Corinthians 15:33: "Do not be deceived: Evil company corrupts good habits."

Proverbs 13:20: "He who walks with wise men will be wise, but the companion of fools will be destroyed."

Questions to Ponder

1. Jehoiada had to engage in strategic planning in order to secure a preferred future. There were a lot of moving parts, and the future of the nation depended upon the hidden baby Joash ascending to the throne. As such, Jehoiada executed his plan with precise timing and expert planning. His devotion to God was matched by his ability to engage in strategic planning. How do you plan for the future? As you think about the future, do you unite your devotion to God with a strategic mind-set?

2. After Joash became king, he wanted to make repairs to the temple. Having spent the first several years of his life

hidden away in the temple, one can understand his affinity for it. However, his source of revenue for these repairs was misguided, and the needed funds did not accumulate. Joash met with the high priest Jehoiada and decided to put a chest at the temple so people could make free will offerings. This solution was a huge success, and they collected more than enough money. In spite of his disappointment, Joash reacted in a reasonable way with Jehoiada. The solution was arrived at with no collateral damage. How well do you react when your expectations fall short? Are you able to impose a reasonable solution when your initial one fails? Do you treat those under you with respect?

3. Joash was another king who undid his life's work before he died. After Jehoiada died, Joash listened to bad counsel, and he fell into idolatry. In his anger, he consented to the death of a prophet sent to him by God. When the Syrian army challenged Joash, he resorted to bribery. He looted the very temple he had refurbished in order to try to pay off the invading army. His poor choices destroyed the good that he had done earlier in life. Have you known someone who made bad choices later in life? How did these choices affect their legacy?

Chapter 5

Amaziah

Read 2 Kings 14 and 2 Chronicles 25.

Amaziah was the ninth ruler of the southern kingdom of Judah. The previous four rulers had not ended well. Jehoram died a violent death of an intestinal disease because of God's judgment. Ahaziah was assassinated by Jehu. The pretender Athalia was killed in a coup that reinstated the rightful succession of power. Finally, Joash, Amaziah's dad, was assassinated in his bed by a couple of his servants. His death was payback for killing the prophet Zechariah. So, with this history, one can imagine the trepidation with which Amaziah assumed the throne.

Amaziah began his reign by doing the right thing. In accordance to the law of God, he executed the servants who killed his father, but he did not kill their children. This action was done in compliance with Deuteronomy 24:16. However, there was a very interesting caveat that preceded Amaziah's actions. Scripture says that Amaziah "did what was right in the sight of the LORD, but not with a loyal heart" (2 Chronicles 25:2). He did not serve God wholeheartedly. He was not all in. His disposition stood in contrast to the Shema. "Hear, O Israel: The LORD is our God, the LORD is one! You shall love the LORD you God with all your heart, with all your soul, and with all your strength" (Deuteronomy 6:4–5). His love for God was not necessarily his motivation for doing right. Right actions that originate from an uncommitted heart can be expected to change when the environment changes. Perhaps his actions were motivated more out of fear and a lack of confidence. This internal condition sets the stage for a change of heart when self-confidence meets a new opportunity.

Don't Throw Good Money after Bad

Earlier in life, I remember a conversation I had with a friend concerning a young lady who was engaged to be married. It seems that the fiancé had proven himself to be an unworthy young man. Let's just say he had some issues with the police. It was evident that this young lady was going to marry a man of trouble. When some friends suggested to the father that he should encourage his daughter to break off the engagement, he responded by saying that he had already spent too much money on the wedding to call it off. Think about it. He would rather his daughter enter an extremely troubled marriage than lose money on the wedding ceremony. Some people refuse to pull out of a bad deal because they are too heavily invested. They would rather lose more money than to cut and run. King Amaziah was faced with such a dilemma.

As Amaziah took hold of his authority as the new king, he began to strengthen the nation's defenses. As he issued the call to arms, the fighting men in Judah numbered only three hundred thousand. The army size was significantly smaller than those of previous generations—so small it could almost be considered alarming given the precariousness of Judah's borders. In order to bolster his military, Amaziah hired one hundred thousand mercenaries from the northern kingdom of Israel. This pragmatic move seemed to make sense, except that God did not want the king to have any such affiliations with their cousins to the north. This opinion was expressed through the words of a prophet who was sent by God to the king to voice His displeasure. The prophet told Amaziah that he was not to let the army of Israel go with him to battle because God was not with Israel. However, if he insisted on taking them with him in battle, he was left with these sobering words: "But if you go, be gone! Be strong in battle! Even so, God shall make you fall before the enemy; for God has power to help and to overthrow" (2 Chronicles 25:8). In other words, go and give it your best try, but you will not succeed because God will be against your efforts.

Amaziah had a serious concern as he contemplated obeying the prophet's words. What about the money he had already paid the mercenaries from the northern kingdom? He was out one hundred talents of silver. Who was going to make up for that loss? The prophet calmly replied with these soothing words of reassurance: "The LORD is able to give you much more than this" (2 Chronicles 25:9). Obediently, Amaziah dismissed the mercenaries, and they did not take it well. As a matter of fact, on their way out of the nation they raided cities and killed three thousand of Amaziah's subjects. Undaunted, Amaziah proceeded to the battle with the Edomites, and God granted him a huge victory. Unfortunately, Amaziah made an astonishing wrong move. He brought the idols of the Edomites back to Judah and worshipped them. As crazy as it sounds, Amaziah worshipped the gods of the army that he just defeated instead of the God who had just given him the victory. His actions were not lost on the prophet who was sent to rebuke him. The prophet said, "Why have you sought the gods of the people, which could not rescue their own people from your hand?" (2 Chronicles 25:15). Amaziah had broken the first two commandments (Exodus 20:1–6), and he didn't even bat an eye. God had given him a huge victory, and he responded by running headlong into idolatry.

Remember, Amaziah has done the right thing up to this point but not with a loyal heart. He was not all in. He was cocky after a great military victory, and his true heart began to reveal itself. He questioned the prophet's right to offer him counsel and threatened to kill him. The prophet agreed to shut up but not before he uttered this last statement: "I know that God has determined to destroy you because you have done this and have not heeded my advice" (2 Chronicles 25:16).

Some people who seem to be humble really aren't. It's just a lack of self-confidence. Give them some measure of success, and what is really in their hearts will be revealed. They do right not from the heart but because it seems to be the safest option. When they get confident, then the true heart is revealed, and it is not pretty. For Amaziah, doing right was not a conviction. It just felt more comfortable. Then he thought he could do things his way. To Amaziah, his way felt more comfortable than God's way. He took it from there, and God let him have his own way.

Have It Your Way

The hamburger chain Burger King used to advertise themselves as the place where "you can have it your way." They even had a catchy little jingle that went like this: "Hold the pickles, hold the lettuce, special orders don't upset us, all we ask is that you let us do it your way."[40] Now, that philosophy may work out well when you want a hamburger, but it is not the way you should approach your walk with God. Here's God's advice about what happens when you want to do life your own way: "Because they hated knowledge and did not choose the fear of the LORD, they would have none of my counsel and despised my every rebuke. Therefore, they shall eat the fruit of their own way and be filled to the full with their own fancies" (Proverbs 1:29–31). Amaziah unfortunately experienced the harsh reality that comes when we are forced to eat the fruit of our own ways. Years earlier, his kingly ancestor Solomon had penned these words: "Pride goes before destruction, and a haughty spirit before a fall" (Proverbs 16:18).

---

[40] https://www.youtube.com/watch?v=eejA2HF5-EQ.

Stay in Your Place

Growing up, there was a pecking order established early among the guys. This hierarchy was reinforced through power and intimidation when needed. It seemed as though everyone sort of knew where they fit in. However, there were those times when a guy would try to elevate himself by challenging someone higher on the totem pole. I vividly remember one such occasion. The confrontation took place on the football field after school. The smaller guy was bound and determined to fight a much tougher adversary. Everyone except the challenger knew it would not end well. I can still remember the sound of fists hitting human flesh. It was a sickening thud. However, the smaller guy would not stop, even though he was being thoroughly humiliated. He actually thought he had a chance. The bigger guy really wasn't even trying. He would literally call his shots before he landed them. Finally, the smaller challenger's friends convinced him to stop. As expected, nobody changed positions on the totem pole. Amaziah also made the mistake of challenging a much stronger adversary, and needless to say, it did not end well.

Pride Goes before a Fall

In his prideful state, Amaziah refused to listen to the advice of others. First, Amaziah refused to listen to the words of the prophet. Then he refused to listen to the words of his opponent. He only listened to the yes-men with whom he had surrounded himself. In his pride, he picked a fight with a bigger guy, Jehoash, the king of

Israel. At this time, the army of Israel was vastly superior to that of Judah. King Jehoash told Amaziah that he needed to stay at home. He was picking a fight with the wrong guy. Amaziah stubbornly refused to listen. So, Amaziah and Jehoash met in battle, and it was no contest. Not only was Amaziah defeated handily in battle, but he was also captured. As if to add insult to injury, the victorious King Jehoash broke down six hundred feet of the wall that surrounded Jerusalem, and he took Amaziah's money in his palace, as well as the gold and the silver in the temple. When Jehoash left town, he took Amaziah back with him to the northern kingdom. The prideful Amaziah was now a trophy in another king's trophy case. Many believe that Amaziah was not released until Jehoash's death.[41] Once Amaziah was able to return to Jerusalem, his own servants plotted against him. When he discovered this plot, he went into exile, only to be hunted down and executed. The man who initially served God but not with a loyal heart was dead. His pride had led to his demise. Now, his son, Uzziah, would ascend to the throne.

Lesson to Learn

From Amaziah's life, we learn the danger of doing the right thing but for the wrong reason. Scripture says that Amaziah did what was right but not with a loyal heart. His heart and his hands were not in sync with the Lord. He did right but not from

[41] Warren Wiersbe, *Be Distinct: Standing Firmly against the World's Tides* (Colorado Springs, CO; David C. Cook 2002), p. 135.

the right motivation. For Amaziah, doing right seemed to be the safest option at the time. However, once he experienced success, he became prideful, and what was really in his heart came out in his actions. Our motivation for doing right must be connected to our walk with Christ. We must choose to do right not because we view it as the safest option but because it glorifies God. Our hearts and our hands must be in agreement. Otherwise, when conditions change, so will our actions.

Verses to Memorize

Mark 12:30: "And you shall love the LORD your God with all your heart, with all your soul, with all your mind, and with all your strength. This is the first commandment."

James 4:8: "Draw near to God and He will draw near to you. Cleanse your hands, you sinners; and purify your hearts, you double-minded."

Questions to Ponder

1. The prophet told Amaziah not to let the hired mercenaries from the northern kingdom accompany him into battle. God was not in this alliance. However, Amaziah objected because he had shilled out one hundred talents of silver. The prophet told Amaziah that the Lord would be against him if he proceeded any further. He did not need to throw good money after bad. It was time to cut and run. Fortunately,

Amaziah admitted his mistake and took the advice of the prophet, and God granted him a military victory. Are you able to stop in the middle of a bad choice and go back in the right direction? Are you too stubborn to admit you have made a bad decision?

2. We are told that Amaziah did not have a loyal heart. He did the right thing because he thought it was the safest option. However, once he became successful, his true heart of pride was revealed. Subsequently, he experienced a downturn in fortune. How loyal is your heart to God? Do you do the right thing because it seems like the safest option, or do you do it to honor God?

3. Pride obscures our vision. It leads us to trust ourselves more than we trust God. The outcome is never good. In what areas of your life do you struggle with pride? How can you choose humility? Is it a one-time decision, or does it require a daily commitment?

Chapter 6

Uzziah

Read 2 Kings 15:1–7 and 2 Chronicles 26.

Let Me Take the Last Shot

Scottie Pippen was one of the all-time greatest players in the history of the NBA. During the Chicago Bulls' golden decade of the 1990s in which they won six championships, he was Michael Jordan's right-hand man. However, during the 1994 Eastern Conference semifinals, an event occurred that put a stain on his otherwise sterling career. The Bulls were playing without Jordan, who had decided to pursue a brief baseball career. They were tied with the New York Knicks at 102 with 1.8 seconds left on the clock. Coach Phil Jackson set up a play for rookie Toni Kukoc to take the final shot. Pippen was incensed that he was overlooked. He was so upset that he said, "I'm tired of this," and refused to enter the game while he sat at the end of the bench.[42] The game continued, and Kukoc took the final shot and made it. The home crowd erupted as the Bulls won the game. However, Pippen could not fully join in on the celebration. He had committed a cardinal sin in sports. He thought he was bigger than the game.

Entitlement Mentality

There have been many articles written about the millennial generation. This generation consists of those who were born between 1980 and 2000. Many consider these individuals to be the most entitled generation ever, and according to *Time* magazine contributor Joel Stein, there is plenty of evidence to back it up. These millennials are so sure of themselves that they think they have the innate ability to determine morality based upon what they feel. Stein writes, "They're so convinced of their own greatness that the National Study of Youth and Religion found the guiding morality of 60% of millennials in any situation is that they'll just be able to feel what's right."[43] One could surmise that the millennials feel entitled to their own sense of morality. Now, that's not to say that this entitlement mentality is the exclusive domain of one generation. It just appears that this generation was raised in an environment that fostered a more me-centric view of the universe.

[42] https://www.basketballnetwork.net/1994-scottie-pippen-refuses-play-the-last-1-8-seconds-of-playoff-game-against-the-knicks-because-the-play-wasnt-designed-for-him/.

[43] http://time.com/247/millennials-the-me-me-me-generation/.

When someone has such thoughts as *I am indispensable,* or *I am God's gift to the world,* or *I have been so successful that what applies to others does not apply to me,* such a person is a prime candidate to possess an entitlement mentality. We also use words and phrases such as pride, an inflated ego, or a big head in connection with such an individual. It stands to reason if success is not handled properly, the successful person begins to overemphasize his or her own importance, steps across a forbidden boundary, and forfeits the honor that he or she could have had. Success can be dangerous. That was evident with the previous king Amaziah. Success reveals the level of loyalty that exists within our hearts, and it can destroy a person who is not equipped to handle it. That is why oftentimes God will humble people before He honors them (Proverbs 15:33).

Uzziah (also known as Azariah) came onto the scene after his father, Amaziah, was defeated and humiliated by Jehoash king of Israel. During the defeat, a six-hundred-foot section of the wall around Jerusalem was torn down, the temple was looted, and Amaziah was taken hostage to the northern kingdom. Uzziah saw firsthand the destruction that pride brought into his father's life and by association into the life of the nation of Judah. Lesson learned? We'll see.

Uzziah became king when he was sixteen years old. He reigned for fifty-two years. He was the legitimate ruler of Judah. He sat on the throne of David in the city of Jerusalem. Upon his ascension to the throne, he began to rebuild the nation's psyche. He sought God early on while he was under the influence of the wise advisor Zechariah. Scripture makes clear that his prosperity was tied directly to his devotion to God. Second Chronicles 26:5 says, "As long as he sought the LORD, God made him prosper."

Under Uzziah's leadership, the nation's boundaries and trade routes were restored. As a result, the nation's economy began to rebound. On the military front, Uzziah defeated the Philistines to reassert control of the major trade route for international commerce. As a measure of security, he rebuilt the missing six-hundred-foot section of the wall around Jerusalem, and he added defensive towers. Additionally, he dug wells, expanded agriculture and livestock, and reorganized and modernized the military. His efforts led to a much safer capital. However, it must be noted that God helped him in what he did. Scripture says that Uzziah was "marvelously helped" by God. As a result, he became strong, and his fame spread.

It is easy to see how Uzziah could be given over to pride if he did not keep himself grounded in his faith. He was extremely successful. Everything he did prospered. He was getting famous around the region among other nations. However, the source of his success was not his ability or his ingenuity. It was God, and unfortunately, he forgot it! When he got strong, he forgot what it was all about. He thought he was the purpose. He thought it was all about him. He overemphasized his own importance and forgot the source of his strength. In his pride, he made a step too far, and he paid the price.

There were three offices in the Old Testament: prophet, priest, and king. A priest could become a prophet, such as Ezekiel and Zachariah, but a prophet or a king could not become a priest. When God gave the law to Moses, He stipulated that only those from the lineage of Aaron, Moses's brother, could be priests. Only the priests could offer sacrifices and burn incense in the tabernacle and later in the temple. More specifically, only the high priest could burn incense on the golden altar each morning and evening. Past attempts to usurp this command did not end well. Just look at what happened to Korah and Dathan in Numbers 16. The earth opened up and swallowed them alive.

MCI Bernard Ebbers

In the 1990s, a surprising leader arose in the telecommunications industry. Dubbed the "telecom cowboy," Bernard Ebbers was not your typical CEO. Ebbers was a transplant Canadian living the southern lifestyle in Mississippi. He was a Southern Baptist Sunday school teacher who wore blue jeans and a big cowboy hat.[44] So his rise to power was most unusual. After starting out as the owner of several hotels, he helped to create a very successful long-distance communications company. Through a series of acquisitions, he eventually found himself as the head of one of the world's largest telecommunications companies, Worldcom MCI. As a successful CEO, he amassed a rather large personal fortune. However, despite all his personal charisma and bold moves, his world eventually fell apart. His fall was so great that *Time* magazine ranks Ebbers as one of the top ten most crooked

---

[44] https://www.theguardian.com/business/2005/mar/16/corporatefraud. usnews.

CEOs of all time.[45] In his effort to handle mounting business losses, Ebbers orchestrated an elaborate $11 billion accounting fraud.[46] After being found guilty, he was sentenced to twenty-five years in prison. Former federal prosecutor Robert Mintz made this observation about Ebbers and other CEOs who have followed a similar path: "There's something to the argument that people who have blazed their own paths in their industries start to believe they don't have to play by the same rules as everyone else."[47] As usual, this line of thinking leads to a great fall.

If you could do a case study on those who fell at the pinnacle of their success, you would more than likely find a common theme: an entitlement mentality. These individuals develop overinflated opinions of themselves. They are the exception. They are indispensable, and, in their pride, they get careless and cross a line that should never be crossed. Unfortunately, Uzziah fits this scenario perfectly. He thought he was the exception. After all, he had an impressive résumé, and everyone was telling him he was an awesome king. What applied to others did not apply to him. In his pride, he thought there was a special dispensation for him. However, Uzziah could not have been more wrong. His ego had clouded his judgment, and his actions sealed his fate.

Here is how the Bible describes what Uzziah did: "But when he was strong his heart was lifted up to his destruction, for he

---

[45] http://content.time.com/time/specials/packages/article/0,28804,1903155_1903156_1903277,00.html.

[46] http://money.cnn.com/2005/07/13/news/newsmakers/ebbers_sentence/.

[47] http://www.nydailynews.com/archives/news/piggies-market-biz-titans-cashed-costing-article-1.479542.

transgressed against the LORD his God by entering the temple of the LORD to burn incense on the altar of incense" (2 Chronicles 26:16). Uzziah went where he did not belong. Once he was in the temple, the high priest and eighty other priests confronted him. The high priest rebuked the king for his action with these words: "It is not for you, Uzziah, to burn incense to the LORD but for the priests, the sons of Aaron, who are consecrated to burn incense. Get out of the sanctuary, for you have trespassed! You shall have no honor from the LORD God" (2 Chronicles 2:18). When Uzziah heard these words from the mouth of the high priest, there was no contrition. There was no repentance. There was only anger. How dare the high priest speak to the king in such a manner. However, before Uzziah could utter a word, leprosy broke out on his forehead. The priests immediately ushered him out of the temple and sent him to live the rest of his days as a leper in isolation. He could no longer go out in public, much less make an appearance at the temple.

Because of his pride, Uzziah lost it all. The last ten years of his life were spent living alone—no more palace, no more festivities, no more royal processions. It was over. As quickly as his honor came, it departed. Even in death, his stigma remained. His epithet read, "He is a leper" (2 Chronicles 26:23). In spite of his earlier success, Uzziah's actions born out of pride diminished his name and his legacy.

Lesson to Learn

Uzziah thought he was a special case. Because of his success as a king, he thought he was above the law. What applied to others did not apply to him. So, in his pride, he stepped across a line he should have never stepped across, and as a result, he forfeited the honor that could have been his. We must never allow pride to make us think we are better than everyone else. We must never think that what applies morally and ethically to others does not apply to us. Regardless of our level of success, we must live with humility and integrity. Otherwise, we are setting ourselves up for a great fall.

Verses to Memorize

Proverbs 16:18: "Pride goes before destruction, and a haughty spirit before a fall."

Romans 12:16: "Be of the same mind toward one another. Do not set your mind of high things, but associate with the humble. Do not be wise in your own opinion."

Questions to Ponder

1. Uzziah made the tragic mistake of overemphasizing his own importance. He thought he was above the rules. Tragically, he was wrong, and it cost him dearly. Is there any area in your

life in which you think you are above the rules? Do you think you can do what others cannot do and get away with it?

2. Uzziah stepped across a forbidden line. He tried to usurp the role of the priest. Are you about to step across a forbidden line? Have the moral and ethical boundaries in your life started to get blurry?

3. Because he transgressed, Uzziah forfeited the honor that could have been his. His reputation was tarnished, and he spent the rest of his life as an ostracized leper. The honor had departed. Are you willing to forfeit the honor that could be yours? Do you need to think about the consequences of your potential actions before you do them?

Chapter 7

Hezekiah

Read 2 Kings 18–20 and 2 Chronicles 29–32.

T he next two kings could not be more different from each other. Jotham was twenty-five years old when he became king. Scripture says that "he did what was right in the sight of the LORD ... but still the people acted corruptly" (2 Chronicles 27:2). He built cities and fought battles. However, after sixteen years on the throne, he died. Unfortunately, the next king did not share his strong faith. King Ahaz instead followed the ways of the kings of Israel. He offered his children as burnt sacrifices to pagan deities (2 Chronicles 28:3), and he encouraged "moral decline in Judah" (2 Chronicles 28:19). Because of his unfaithfulness, God allowed the Syrians and the Assyrians to defeat him. His loss was great, but he still refused to turn to the Lord. And in his most brazen act of defiance, Ahaz cut up the articles of the temple and shut its doors. Then he erected pagan altars for himself throughout Jerusalem. Ahaz provoked God to anger, and his reign was ended after sixteen years. Needless to say, the nation was once again in disarray and in need of a reformer king. That was when Hezekiah came to the throne.

Reformation Brings Religious and Political Upheaval

Martin Luther is perhaps the greatest reformer of all time. His relentless writings spearheaded the reformation of the Christian Church in the early 1500s. At a time when the Catholic Church and their popes dominated the religious and political landscape of Europe, this Augustinian monk had the courage to stand up and risk his life for the sake of reforming the wayward church. On October 31, 1517, Luther posted his famous 95 Theses on the door of the church at Witttenberg, Germany.[48] These grievances called out the teachings of the Catholic Church as well as the actions of the pope. Not only did his efforts lead to the greatest schism in church history, they also caused wars and conflicts such as the German Peasant's War and the Thirty-Year War.[49] When reformation changes the religious and political fabric, there is usually pushback, and things can turn violent. The Jewish king Hezekiah brought religious reformation to the nation, and his efforts upset the geopolitical climate of the day.

Hezekiah began his reign in 715 BC and immediately brought about reforms to the troubled nation. Scripture simply says that

---

[48] https://www.history.com/this-day-in-history/martin-luther-posts-95-theses.
[49] https://theconversation.com/five-of-the-most-violent-moments-of-the-reformation-71535.

"he did what was right in the sight of the LORD." He removed the vestiges of institutionalized idolatry that his father, Ahaz, had established. Also, he opened the temple for worship again and repaired it. To ensure that true worship would be restored in Jerusalem, he spoke these poignant words to the priests:

> Hear me, Levites! Now sanctify yourselves, sanctify the house of the LORD God of your fathers, and carry out the rubbish from the holy place. For our fathers have trespassed and done evil in the eyes of the LORD our God; they have forsaken Him, have turned their faces away from the dwelling place of the LORD, and turned their backs to Him. They have also shut up the doors of the vestibule, put out the lamps, and have not burned incense or offered burnt offerings in the holy place to the God of Israel. Therefore, the wrath of the LORD fell upon Judah and Jerusalem, and He has given them up to trouble, to desolation, and to jeering, as you see with our eyes. For indeed, because of this our fathers have fallen by the sword; and our sons, our daughters, and our wives are in captivity. Now it is in my heart to make a covenant with the LORD God of Israel, that His fierce wrath may turn away from us My sons, do not be negligent now, for the LORD has chosen you to stand before Him, to

serve Him, and that you should minister to Him
and burn incense. (2 Chronicles 29:5–11)

Without a doubt, Hezekiah was realigning the nation, and
it should be noted that his initial moves were met with success.
His total commitment to God changed business as usual. His
devotion to God led him to change the nation's habits and to
break away from a lesser lifestyle. This fervent commitment to
God emboldened Hezekiah to rebel against the Assyrians by
defeating their vassal state of Philistia. His commitment led him
to remove idols and to reinstitute the Passover. He took the people
back to where they needed to be with God. His reforms positively
impacted the lives of others. His changes were bold and put the
nation in a position where the people once again had to learn to
trust God. However, as is often the case, when we realign our lives
with God, we face conflict.

Seven years prior to Hezekiah taking the throne, the northern
kingdom of the Jews had been defeated by the ruthless Assyrians.
After their defeat, the Jews in the north were dispersed throughout
the Assyrian Empire. This relocation decimated the Jewish fabric
of the northern kingdom. The Assyrians were the established
superpower of the day, and Hezekiah had rebelled against them.
In his zeal to follow God, he had grabbed a tiger by the tail, and
now he was going to have to deal with the consequences.

Survival 101

There is an interesting magazine called *How to Survive Anything*. In our day of constant apocalyptic themed movies and TV series, a magazine such as this is assured a healthy readership. In its 2018 edition, topics included how to survive natural disasters, terrorist attacks, animal attacks, and even an artificial intelligence takeover. Readers are told how to prepare and how to survive in the worst-case scenarios. There is even a list of the most apocalypse-ready cities in America. In case you are interested, the best city to live in post nuclear apocalypse according to realtor.com is Kansas City, Missouri.[50] The nation of Judah was facing an impending disaster. They were going to be attacked by the most powerful empire in the world. With an invasion imminent, everyone was thinking about survival.

It took several years for Assyria to be able to deal with Hezekiah's revolt because they had been battling with the Babylonians in the east.[51] However, in 701 BC, the Assyrian king Sennacherib was ready to put Hezekiah and the defiant Jewish kingdom in their place. He began by conquering forty-six fortified cities in Judah. As Sennacherib descended upon Jerusalem, Hezekiah had an "uh-oh" moment. It's one of those "what have I gotten myself into" times of life. So, he sent words of apology to Sennacherib. He said, "I have done wrong; turn away from me; whatever you

---

[50] *How to Survive Anything*. 2018 edition. Centennial Media New York, NY. 2018, p. 93. Michael Fleeman, editor.

[51] Paul R. House, *New American Commentary: 1, 2 Kings* (Nashville, TN, Broadman Press, 1995), 360.

impose I will pay" (2 Kings 18:14). Think about it. Hezekiah was apologizing to a pagan king for doing right. He was willing to pay whatever price Sennacherib told him to pay. So, Sennacherib gave him a bill of three hundred talents of silver and thirty talents of gold. This was an exorbitant amount. Consequently, Hezekiah had to liquidate everything in order to pay the bill. He got all the money out of the temple. He even had to strip the gold off the temple doors as well as from the pillars in the temple.

Bold moves are often challenged, and we are forced to decide whether we will go forward and trust God or whether we will go back into some form of bondage. Admittedly, the circumstances can look pretty overwhelming. Hezekiah's first response was to cave. However, he was forced to decide whether and how much he would trust God. It is easy to be bold for God when we are not challenged. What happens, however, when we are challenged? How long will we last? Do you apologize for following God, or do you stand your ground?

Nuts

The Battle of the Bulge was one of the bloodiest battles that the United States Army had to fight during World War II. In December 1944, Allied commanders thought that the war was basically over, and the Germans were retreating into Germany. The Normandy Invasion had initiated a series of battles that the Germans seemed to be unable to recover from. Unbeknownst to Allied Commander General Dwight Eisenhower, Adolf Hitler had planned a massive counteroffensive against the allies through the Ardennes Forest in Belgium. The ensuing German offensive would become known as the Battle of the Bulge. During the height of the battle, the strategic Belgium town of Bastogne was being held by the 101st Airborne Division under the command of General Anthony McAuliffe. Surrounded and vastly outnumbered by German forces, McAuliffe was given the opportunity to surrender. His audacious written response was given in one word: "nuts."[52] McAuliffe's only hope rested in the hard-charging efforts of "old blood and guts" General George Patton and the US Third Army. Fortunately, Patton was the man for the job. One historian notes, "There was no other man in the Army that could have done that. No one else had the willpower and knowledge of the terrain. He turned the entire 3rd Army 90 degrees and headed north about 200,000 men and 200 tanks. It took the sheer willpower of Patton."[53] Patton broke through the German lines in record time and saved Bastogne and the 101st Airborne Division from annihilation. Like Bastogne, Hezekiah and Jerusalem were also surrounded by superior forces and given an opportunity to surrender. However, there was no earthly general barreling to their rescue.

As Hezekiah was surrounded by the Assyrian army, he was faced with circumstantial and theological confusion. The Assyrian king Sennacherib sent three of his field commanders to Jerusalem to issue a call for its surrender. In response, Hezekiah dispatched

---

[52] Bill O'Reilly, *Killing Patton*. 2014, Henry Holt and Company LLC, New York, NY. p. 124.

[53] https://www.investors.com/news/management/leaders-and-success/general-george-patton-towered-at-the-bulge/.

three of his own representatives to talk with these Assyrians. The spokesman for the Assyrian army ridiculed the Jewish revolt led by Hezekiah. He made light of any reliance the Jews might have upon a friendly intervention by the Egyptians. He capped it off by saying that trusting in the Lord was futile. He further stated that the altars that Hezekiah tore down in Jerusalem were actually the altars where God wanted to be worshipped. Hezekiah had offended God by tearing down these pagan altars, and now God was going to punish the Jews for his transgression.

A Word to the Wise

Be careful about taking theological advice from someone who is far from God. The Assyrian was telling the people that if Hezekiah had continued in idolatry like his predecessor, then there would be no problem. In other words, Hezekiah's religious reforms were wrong, and they displeased God. He even claimed that God instructed him to "Go up against this land and destroy it" (2 Kings 18:25). It's difficult when someone tells you that something you have done for God is wrong and that God is going to punish you for doing it.

The words of the Assyrian were so discouraging that the Jewish representatives asked him to speak in the diplomatic language of the day (Aramaic) instead of Hebrew. They did not want the people of Jerusalem to hear him and get discouraged. However, the spokesman refused their plea and continued to attack Hezekiah in Hebrew. He even said that the people listening to his words would consume their own feces and drink their own urine in order to try to survive the coming Assyrian onslaught. The Assyrian said, "Do not let Hezekiah deceive you, for he shall not be able to deliver you from his hand; nor let Hezekiah make you trust in the LORD, saying, 'the LORD will surely deliver us; this city shall not be given into the hand of the king of Assyria'" (2 Kings 18:29–30). Hezekiah had told the people to trust God. Sennacherib had the arm of the flesh, but they had the Lord to fight their battles. Now, the Assyrian offered a way out. If the Jews surrendered, he would let them stay in the land until he was ready to relocate them to new cities within the Assyrian Empire.

There are those who seek to undermine your faith and trust in God. They tell you to do what is most expedient or what seems to be most practical. In other words, don't trust God; trust them. However, you must be committed to stay connected to God's purpose and follow godly advice. The men brought the words of the Assyrians to Hezekiah, and there was much weeping. It looked like a truly hopeless situation. However, Hezekiah humbled himself and tore his garments. He sent his men to seek advice from the prophet Isaiah. Isaiah told them to tell Hezekiah not to fear the king of Assyria. God would send a spirit of fear upon him, and he would hear a rumor and return to his own land, where he would eventually die.

You Need Somebody Who Can Give You Good Advice

Everybody needs to have a go-to person for words of advice or encouragement. Often, this nugget of advice or encouragement sets the stage for lifelong success. At the outbreak of the first

Persian Gulf War in 1991, Billy Graham was summoned to the White House for prayer and spiritual guidance. President George H. W. Bush said that Graham's presence reassured him of the "moral clarity of our mission that January night."[54] Like President Bush, we need someone we can go to during these uncertain times. Someone who can pray for us. Someone who can reassure us that we are on the right track. Fortunately, Hezekiah had one of the greatest prophets of all time who could pray for him and instruct him in the ways of God.

As Isaiah had predicted, the Assyrians heard of greater military concerns and had to leave. The king of Assyria was informed that the king of Ethiopia was coming up the coast of Philistia to aid the city of Ekron. So, he had to divert his forces from assaulting Jerusalem. As such, Sennacherib sent another message to Jerusalem to let the city know that the delay of their destruction was not an act of God. He would be back, and he would destroy them. It was still futile for them to trust in God. When Hezekiah received this letter, he went to the temple to pray. In this prayer, he acknowledged God's greatness and asked God to hear his request. He acknowledged the severity of the crisis he faced. He requested help because God's honor was at stake. He wanted God to be worshipped. In response to his prayer, Isaiah sent word to Hezekiah that God had answered his prayer and that Sennacherib would never enter the city. Subsequently, God sent an angel to decimate the Assyrian army. The Assyrians were

---

[54] http://www.chicagotribune.com/news/sns-bc-us--billy-graham-presidents-20180222-story.html.

forced to retreat. Years later, Sennacherib was killed by two of his own sons in a coup. He never entered Jerusalem.

Don't Get Careless

There are events that occur in our lives that have a way of shaping our future. So much is out of our control. Sometimes, there are needs that are so great that we know only God can meet them. At other times, we face dangers, and because of our lack of spiritual preparation, we don't see them. Hezekiah faced two dangers: death and pride. With one, he was successful, and with the other, he fell prey. That is why it is vitally important that we never take time off spiritually. How many people have succumbed to temptation during a time of ease or during a time when they were basking in a victory?

Second Kings 20:1 starts out with these sobering words: "In those days Hezekiah became sick and was at the point of death." Hezekiah had been a good king. He led his people back to righteousness, and they experienced amazing military success. However, he was sick. The situation was so dire that the prophet Isaiah showed up. Instead of pronouncing a miraculous cure, he spoke these ominous words to the king: "Thus, says the LORD, set your house in order, for you shall die; you shall not recover" (2 Kings 20:1). In other words, make sure your will is up to date because you are going to die. Remember, Isaiah was a true prophet of God. If he said you were going to die, then you were going to die.

Hezekiah was completely undone. He turned his face to the

wall, so no one could see him, and he prayed. In his prayer, he asked God for more time. He referred to his own character, God's mercy, and his track record as king. The nation still faced a threat from Assyria. There were still those who wanted to lead the nation back into idolatry. Hezekiah had stood strong, and he asked for more time. While Hezekiah was praying, Isaiah was exiting the palace, but before he could get out, the Lord spoke to him with these words: "Turn back, and say to Hezekiah the leader of my people, thus says the LORD, the God of David your father: I have heard your prayer, I have seen your tears. Behold, I will heal you. On the third day you shall go up to the house of the LORD, and I will add fifteen years to your life. I will deliver you and this city out of the hand of the king of Assyria, and I will defend this city for my own sake and for my servant David's sake" (2 Kings 20:5–6). Hezekiah would get a fifteen-year reprieve, and the city would be kept safe from the Assyrians. God answered this prayer for His own sake and for the sake of the promise He had made to David. Hezekiah was to live for God's purposes and not his own. He was around forty years old when the extension of life was given.

As part of God's remedy, Isaiah used the medicine of the day and applied it to Hezekiah's sore. In response to Isaiah's words and actions, Hezekiah asked for a sign that would confirm his healing. This request was well within reason. His father, Ahaz, was told to ask for a sign concerning the prophecy given to him by Isaiah. He didn't comply, but the sign was given anyway in Isaiah 7:14, "Therefore, the LORD Himself will give you a sign: Behold, the virgin shall conceive and bear a Son and shall call His name Immanuel." So, Hezekiah felt comfortable asking for a sign, and Isaiah gave him one. The sign happened, and in three days according to the word of Isaiah, Hezekiah was back worshipping in the temple in Jerusalem.

Hezekiah prayed, and God answered not only with more life but with the promise of continual military victory over the Assyrians. Ephesians 3:20 says, "Now to Him who is able to do exceedingly abundantly above all that we ask or think, according to the power that works in us." Jesus said to "keep asking, seeking and knocking." Don't get too worn out to pray and ask. Pray big but have your prayers connected to God's purpose. Hezekiah tried to live for God's purpose and to make a difference. Some things God will do only if we ask.

Taking a Test and You Don't Even Know It

Job interviews are stressful encounters. Applicants must be both prepared and relaxed. Questions are asked, and body language is observed. And to top it off, there are others who are competing for the same position. Recommendations for how to approach a job interview are plentiful on the internet. However, one surprising detail that many overlook is that the interview actually begins when someone gets out of the car. Human resource consultant Kelly Marinelli says, "It's important to be friendly to everyone because with my clients, we ask the receptionist, we ask the parking garage attendant, especially with higher-level roles, was this person respectful to you and friendly?"[55] Applicants are being tested, and they don't even know it. The same was true of Hezekiah. He was about to enter a time of observation and testing, and he was completely unaware.

After Hezekiah's amazing healing experience, there was a dramatic turn of events. Baladan, king of Babylon, sent his envoys to Hezekiah with a letter and a present because he heard that Hezekiah had been sick. Hezekiah was blown away that the king of Babylon would do such a thing. King Baladan had been building himself quite a reputation in the east. He had been battling the Assyrians for years. Even though Babylon was still technically under the dominion of Assyria, it was apparent that Babylon was soon to be the greater power. Unfortunately, Hezekiah let the flattery get to him, and he acted in a very foolish manner. Scripture says, "And Hezekiah welcomed them, and he showed them all the house of his treasure, the silver, the gold, the spices, the precious oil, his armory, all that was found in the storehouses. There was nothing in his house or in all his realm that Hezekiah did not show them" (2 Kings 20:13). He showed them everything he had. All his military and financial assets were put on display for the envoys of Babylon to see. Many believe that Babylon probably wanted to enlist Judah in their rebellion against the Assyrians. They could attack from the west, and Babylon could attack from the east.

Unfortunately, Hezekiah was flattered and blinded by his own pride. The Babylonian visit was actually a test from God

---

[55] https://money.usnews.com/money/careers/interviewing/articles/ job-interview-mistakes-to-avoid.

for the purpose of revealing Hezekiah's heart. Second Chronicles 32:31 says, "And so in the matter of the envoys of the princes of Babylon, who had been sent to him to inquire about the sign that had been done in the land, God left him to himself, in order to test him and to know all that was in his heart." Hezekiah was being tested, and he didn't even have a clue.

Once the envoys left, the prophet Isaiah arrived. When the prophet arrives, something always happens. Sometimes the news is good, and sometimes it is bad. On this occasion, it was terrible. Isaiah asked what Hezekiah had shown to the envoys. Hezekiah said, "Everything." Isaiah responded by telling Hezekiah that one day the Babylonians would come and take everything he had shown them. This was a word of judgment. Hezekiah's pride had clouded his mind. He accepted the inevitability of Isaiah's words, but he was glad that there would at least be peace during his lifetime.

Hezekiah was being tested and didn't even know it. He knew what the stakes were when he was facing death, but he was clueless when he was showing off for the Babylonians. God tested him to reveal his heart. Hezekiah didn't need to form an alliance with the Babylonians. God had already promised to defend the nation. However, he had forgotten about God, and he placed all the emphasis upon himself, and the result was tragic. When he spoke with Isaiah, he referred to "my house" and "my treasures." They weren't his. They belonged to God, and he was just a steward.

A consistent walk connected with the purposes of God is vital because we never know when our faith will be put to the test. It might be through difficulty or it might be through success.

In difficulty, pray big. In success, stay humble and connected to God's purpose. Hezekiah should have told the Babylonian envoys, "Thank you for coming. God is good, and he has done a great work in my life. Would you like to know more about Him?" Instead, he bragged about his stuff. He wasted an incredible opportunity to introduce the Babylonians to the true God.

Lesson to Learn

Hezekiah had an extremely effective prayer life so long as he stayed connected to the purposes of God. His prayers for military victory and for physical healing were answered because they were connected to God's purposes. However, after he received an extra fifteen years of life, Hezekiah became more about himself than about God. In his pride, he showed the Babylonian representatives all "his riches." Even after the prophet Isaiah rebuked him, Hezekiah took comfort that at least there would be peace during his lifetime. He showed little concern for those who would have to deal with his mistake after his death. Hezekiah's example shows us that we must stay connected to the purposes of God. We must remember that we are to live for His kingdom and not our own. Always ask yourself, "If God answered every prayer I am praying right now, how would it impact His kingdom?"

Verses to Memorize

Matthew 6:9–10: "In this manner, therefore, pray: Our Father in heaven, hallowed by Your name. Your kingdom come. Your will be done on earth as it is in heaven."

Matthew 6:33: "But seek first the kingdom of God and His righteousness, and all these things shall be added to you."

Questions to Ponder

1. As Hezekiah and the people were preparing to defend Jerusalem, one of the Assyrian military commanders offered them some theological advice. He was a pagan idolater, yet he was dispensing theological advice to God's people. Of course, his advice was wrong. Are you currently taking theological advice from someone who is far from God? Are you getting moral and ethical advice from someone who does not share your commitment to Christ?

2. During times of crisis, Hezekiah would go to his trusted advisor, the prophet Isaiah. He knew Isaiah was a godly man who listened to God. Do you have anyone you can go to for good godly advice? What is the number one quality that you look for in an advisor? Why?

3. When the ambassadors from Babylon showed up, Hezekiah had no idea he was being tested. His pride clouded his

discernment. As such, he failed the test miserably. A consistent walk of faith is vital because you never know when your faith will be tested either by danger or by success. How do you keep yourself sharp spiritually? Have you ever had a time of testing and you did not realize it until it was over?

Chapter 8

Manasseh

Read 2 Kings 21 and 2 Chronicles 33.

One of the best-loved stories in all English literature is Charles Dickens's *A Christmas Carol*. It's the tale of a miserly old curmudgeon named Ebenezer Scrooge who is visited by three ghosts on Christmas Eve. As he is confronted by the past, made aware of the present, and terrified by the future, Scrooge comes face-to-face with the fact that he must change. As the story unfolds, Dickens does a masterful job describing the transformation of Scrooge's character. Ebenezer Scrooge becomes a loving and generous soul. It's the classic case of someone changing for the good before they die. In the litany of Jewish kings, perhaps no one needed more reformation than the next king, King Manasseh. He was so bad that he was compared to the wicked King Ahab of the defunct northern kingdom. No king before or after was as bad as Manasseh. His wickedness led to horrible consequences for both himself and the nation. However, in the midst of his misery, he changed, though his personal repentance could not undo all of the harm he had inflicted upon the nation.

Manasseh became king after the death of his father, Hezekiah. Many believed that he spent perhaps as many as ten years in a coregency with Hezekiah.[56] Regardless of when his tenure began, Manasseh became the longest reigning king in the history of Judah. He reigned a total of fifty-five years. Not only was he the longest reigning king, he was also the vilest. According to 2 Kings 24:3, "the sins of Manasseh" were the reason that God would not relent on his judgment on the nation of Judah. It seems that Manasseh took wickedness to the next level. He led the Jews to become just like the Canaanites that they had originally dispossessed of the land. His list of sins was legendary. He managed to undo all the good that his father, Hezekiah, had done.

In his wickedness, he rebuilt the altars to Baal, and he led the nation into the worship of the heavenly bodies. He offered his sons as sacrifices to pagan deities as he engaged in sorcery and witchcraft. "He even set a carved image of Asherah that he had made in the house of which the LORD had said to David and to Solomon his son, 'In this house and in Jerusalem, which I have chosen out of all the tribes of Israel, I will put My name forever'" (2 Kings 21:8). By putting the Asherah pole in the temple, he was declaring Asherah to be the wife of Yahweh.[57] His corrupt influence was so pervasive that Judah became more wicked than the Canaanites whom they originally dispossessed of the land (2 Kings 21:9).

---

[56] Warren Wiersbe, Be Distinct. P. 192.

[57] Tony Merida, p. 295.

Failure to Heed the Warning

On May 22, 2011, the town of Joplin, Missouri, was hit by a devastating EF-5 tornado. The powerful storm killed 162 residents and injured hundreds of others. Approximately nine thousand homes and other buildings were destroyed as well.[58] The high casualty rate was due to the fact that many residents failed to heed the severe weather sirens that went off twenty minutes before the storm's arrival. Based upon interviews with citizens, the National Oceanic and Atmospheric Administration concluded that residents had "become desensitized or complacent to sirens."[59] One official added, "This was a warned event."[60] Unfortunately, for whatever reasons, some failed to take action, and the inevitable consequences followed. Manasseh and the citizens of the southern kingdom were given many warnings, and they too failed to take the necessary action.

In the midst of this debauchery, God sent prophets to warn Manasseh and the people of their gross sins, but they did not listen. Even the prophet Isaiah was no match for the corrupt monarch. Many believe that Manasseh was the one responsible for Isaiah being sawn in two. Jewish Rabbinic tradition says that Manasseh hunted down Isaiah because his prophecies concerning the nation enraged the king. In his attempt to avoid the king's wrath, Isaiah

---

[58] https://www.reuters.com/article/us-joplin-tornado-report/many-failed-to-heed-joplin-tornado-warnings-report-says-idUSTRE78J6TJ20110920.

[59] Ibid.

[60] http://www.nbcnews.com/id/44596753/ns/weather/t/most-joplin-residents-ignored-twister-warning-experts-find/#.W0eQpy2ZPq0.

sought refuge in a tree trunk. However, when Isaiah's location was discovered, Manasseh had the tree sawn in two with Isaiah in it.[61] His cruelty and immorality knew no limits—that is, until God sent judgment in the form of the Assyrians.

Because Manasseh would not listen to the prophets, God sent the "captains of the army of the king of Assyria" (2 Chronicles 33:11). The Assyrians were some of the cruelest people in the ancient world. When they arrived, they put hooks in Manasseh's nose and fetters on his feet and took him to Babylon, which at the time served as Assyria's second capital. History records that the Assyrian king Esarhaddon forced vassal kings to serve as his slaves.[62] As such, Manasseh was unceremoniously called into service. However, in his captivity, Manasseh humbled himself before the Lord and repented of his sins. Scripture records Manasseh's contrition with these words: "Now when he was in affliction, he implored the LORD his God, and humbled himself greatly before the God of his fathers and prayed to Him; and he received his entreaty, heard his supplication, and brought him back to Jerusalem into his kingdom. Then Manasseh knew that the LORD was God" (2 Chronicles 33:12–13).

---

[61] Bruce B. Barton, *Life Application Bible Commentary: Hebrews*, (Carol Stream, Il: Tyndale House Publishers), p. 200.

[62] Holman Old Testament Commentary 1 and 2 Chronicles, p. 353.

Rotten Tomatoes

When I was a teenager, I got a job one summer packing tomatoes for a local farmer. The job was simple. After the teenage girls sorted the tomatoes and sent them down the conveyor belt, the guys would put the tomatoes into cardboard boxes and stack them on pallets. When the owner was away, the typical teenage interactions would take place, and bad tomatoes would escape our notice. Consequently, some rotten tomatoes got put into boxes destined for New Jersey. Once these tomatoes arrived, the buyers promptly sent them back. The rotten tomatoes had caused other tomatoes to rot, and the whole truck stunk. We then had to sort back through the boxes of rotten tomatoes and salvage what we could. Needless to say, it was a very unpleasant experience. The influence of Manasseh on the nation of Judah is similar to a rotten tomato. He was corrupt and corrupting. Even though he was removed from the nation, the rot he left behind continued to infest the people.

Once back in Jerusalem, Manasseh began to try to undo all the damage he had inflicted upon the nation. He got the pagan altars out of the temple and the city of Jerusalem. He repaired the Lord's altar and commanded that the people "serve the LORD God of Israel" (2 Chronicles 33:15–16). He even made military improvements. However, all his acts of repentance could not undo the damage that his previous lawlessness had inflicted upon the moral fabric of the nation. Upon his death, his son Amon came to the throne, and in short time, he led the nation back into rampant idolatry.

Even though Manasseh repented and had a changed life, he could not alter all the evil he had brought upon the people. His previous actions had poisoned the soul of the nation. The repercussions of his former ways remained. Remember, personal repentance does not take away the consequences for previous actions. Upon his death, Manasseh's son Amon would ascend to the throne, and the nation would descend back into idolatry. King Amon followed his father's former way of life. Scripture says, "But he did evil in the sight of the LORD, as his father Manasseh had done; for Amon sacrificed to all the carved images which his father Manasseh had made and served them" (2 Chronicles 33:22). Amon was such a disgusting king that his own servants plotted against him, and after only two years on the throne, he was assassinated. All was not well in the southern kingdom.

Lesson to Learn

From Manasseh we learn that personal repentance does not undo all the damage that our sin has inflicted upon the lives of others. In his wickedness, Manasseh poisoned the soul of his family and his nation. Just because he repented and changed did not mean that all the people who were negatively influenced by his sin would also change. Despite his efforts to make things right, his family and his nation did not change. They remained corrupted by his sin. We must always remember that our bad example may lead others astray, and they may never come back. Sin has consequences, and it does produce collateral damage.

Therefore, think about the lives of those you love the most before you get involved with sin.

Verses to Memorize

Proverbs 20:7: "The righteous man walks in his integrity and his children are blessed after him."

Second Timothy 4:7: "I have fought the good fight, I have finished the race, I have kept the faith."

Questions to Ponder

1. Manasseh ignored all the warnings that God sent his way. He refused to listen to God's Word or the prophets. He even had Isaiah sewn in two. Are you currently ignoring any warnings that God might be sending your way? Are you acting against someone who may be trying to help you not to go astray?

2. When internal motivation ceases to be effective, it takes external motivation to get the job done. Manasseh would not heed the call from God's Word to repent. So, God sent an external agent in the form of the Assyrian army. It is always better to choose to do right than be forced to do right. Is there any conviction in your heart that you continually ignore? Does it take external constraints to make you do what you are supposed to do?

3. When Manasseh was in captivity, he repented. Eventually, the Assyrians allowed him to return to Jerusalem. Once he returned, he tried to undo all the damage he had inflicted upon the nation. He was now a changed man. However, he could not undo all the poison he had inflicted upon the moral fabric of the nation during his rebelliousness. Are you currently leading others into some type of sin? Is your example providing cover for those who want to do evil?

Chapter 9

Josiah

Read 2 Kings 22–25 and 2 Chronicles 34–36.

Making the Best of a Lost Cause

There is a popular idiom that people use when someone is making improvements to a sinking ship. It is called "rearranging the deck chairs on the Titanic."[63] This expression gives thought to the utter futility of doing your best for a lost cause. For the nation of Judah, the die had been cast. They were going to be disciplined by God. They were going to be removed from the land. The poison inflicted by the early part of Manasseh's reign had so infected the heart of the nation that only drastic action could bring healing. Judgment was certain. However, into

---

[63] https://www.washingtonpost.com/blogs/arts-post/post/literally-rearranging-the-deck-chairs-on-the-titanic/2012/04/12/gIQAqKhbCT_blog.html?utm_term=.51fa8145a497.

this environment an unexpected king came to the throne. A king with a heart for God. A king who wanted to reform the nation. Regardless of future events, this king was determined to do his best for God. He was determined to lead the nation in a righteous direction. He would do his best on a sinking ship for the glory of God.

Josiah was the last good Jewish king to sit on the throne in Jerusalem. He was crowned king at the tender age of eight. The year was 640 BC, and a lot of change was on the geopolitical horizon. The Assyrian Empire was beginning to show some cracks. These crevices broke open in 627 BC with the death of the Assyrian king Ashurbanipal.[64] The following year, the city of Babylon broke away from their control. In 612 BC, the Assyrian capital of Nineveh fell. Three years later, the Assyrians sought an alliance with the Egyptians in a last-ditch effort to maintain their sovereignty. As the world powers were changing, the tiny Jewish nation was given somewhat of a reprieve. The Assyrians were too weakened in the east to worry about Judah in the west. It was in this setting that an eight-year-old boy became king, and he did extremely well.

We have been given signposts along the way that inform us as to how Josiah's spiritual life developed. Second Chronicles 34:3 says, "For in the eighth year of his reign, while he was still young, he began to seek the God of his father David; and in the twelfth year he began to purge Judah and Jerusalem of the high places, the wooden images, the carved images and the molded

---

[64] Paul R. House, *New American Commentary, 1, 2 Kings*, volume 8. Broadman and Holman Publishers, 1995, p. 381.

images." At sixteen, he had a conversion, and four years later, he began to get rid of the idolatrous junk that inundated the nation. His reforms were thorough. In the eighteenth year of his reign, he gave the word that the temple was to be renovated. Obviously, previous idolatrous kings such as Manasseh and Amon had let the temple fall into disrepair. The twenty-six-year-old king began the process of repairing the temple that had been built hundreds of years earlier by King Solomon. As repairs began, there was an interesting development. A book was found. However, it was not any book. It was the long-neglected book of the law. Most commentators believe that the book mentioned is the book of Deuteronomy.[65] In response to the reading of this book, Josiah was heartbroken. He tore his garments in a sign of repentance, and he commanded the priest to go and to inquire of the Lord as to what all of this meant for him and the nation. In response, Hilkiah and those with him went to a prophetess named Huldah. She basically said that all the curses spoken of in the book would befall the nation, but they would not happen during Josiah's lifetime because he was a righteous king. They brought back word to Josiah, and he began the process of restoring true worship to the nation. As part of the restoration, he reinstituted the Passover.

Don't Mail It In

There have been many false predictions concerning the return of Jesus Christ. For some reason, there are those who think they

---

[65] NAC Vol. 9 J. A. Thompson Broadman and Holman 1994, p. 377.

have been blessed with the inside scoop. However, they all end up deluded and disappointed. Some of those who followed the false predictions of Edgar Whisenant's *88 Reasons Why Jesus Will Come Back in 1988* maxed out their credit cards because they thought they would be raptured and therefore not around to pay back their debt.[66] Such thinking is incredibly misguided. Believers should always live with the awareness of the imminent return of Christ (Titus 2:13). At the end of the book of Revelation, the word *maranatha* is written. This Aramaic word translates "even so come Lord Jesus." It is a cry for the return of Christ to set up His earthly kingdom. The word was used by the early church as a greeting to motivate one another to stay strong in the midst of a dangerous world.[67] So, any discussion of the second coming should motivate people to give their best for God and not just run out the clock. The great Martin Luther was purportedly once asked what he would do if he knew that the world was going to end the next day. In response, he said, "If I knew that the world would end tomorrow, I would plant an apple tree today."[68] This statement should encapsulate the motivation of every believer. Live every day with all you have. Give God your best every day. Josiah knew that the country would be judged by God, yet he did his best to turn the heart of the nation back to God. He did not have a fatalistic attitude like his forefather Hezekiah. He lived as though his actions mattered. And they did!

Josiah successfully reinstituted true worship in Jerusalem. He

---

[66] https://thecitizen.com/2011/05/20/my-last-column/.

[67] https://www.gotquestions.org/maranatha.html.

[68] https://www.luther.de/en/baeume.html.

provided strong leadership. The priests were functioning properly. The temple was fully operational. The visible vestiges of idolatry were diminished. All was well until Pharaoh Necho tried to come though Judah on his way north to meet up with the Assyrians. The year was 609 BC, and the Assyrians and the Egyptians hoped that an alliance between the two would stem the advances of the Babylonians. Josiah went out to confront Necho. The Pharaoh basically told Josiah that this was not his fight and he needed to stay home. Josiah refused to listen, and he disguised himself as a regular soldier and went to war with Necho. In battle, he was fatally wounded. Upon his death, the fate of the Jewish nation was sealed. With Josiah gone, the people began the rapid descent into total defeat. The next twenty-three years witnessed four incredibly weak kings and a loss of sovereignty.

The End of the Kingdom

After Josiah was killed in battle, Judah became the vassal state of Egypt. In their quest to continue the Davidic dynasty, the Jewish people chose Josiah's son Jehoahaz to be their next king. However, after three months on the throne, Pharaoh Necho removed Jehoahaz and replaced him with his brother Jehoiakim, whom he renamed Eliakim. In 605 BC, Egypt and Assyria were defeated by the Babylonians. Under the leadership of their new king, Nebuchadnezzar, the Babylonians promptly invaded Judah. The Jews were now under the dominion of the Babylonians. In 597 BC, Judah rebelled against the Babylonians, and they were conquered once again. King Eliakim was executed, and he was succeeded by his son Jehoiachin. Jehoiachin reigned for only three months and ten days and was taken into Babylonian exile. The crown was then given to Zedekiah, who was Eliakim's brother. After several years on the throne, Zedekiah also rebelled against the Babylonians, and this time Nebuchadnezzar had enough. In 586 BC, the Babylonian army broke through the walls that surrounded Jerusalem. After this breach, King Zedekiah was forced to flee the city with his sons. However, Zedekiah and his sons were captured on the plains of Jericho. Once in custody, the Babylonian soldiers brought Zedekiah and his sons before Nebuchadnezzar. In a callous fashion, Nebuchadnezzar had Zedekiah's sons killed in front of him, and then he gouged out Zedekiah's eyes. The last vision that the last king of Judah had was the death of his royal heirs. Judgment had come. The kingdom had fallen.

Verses to Memorize

Matthew 16:18: "And I say to you that you are Peter, and on this rock I will build My church and the gates of Hades shall not prevail against it."

Acts 1:8: "But you shall receive power when the Holy Spirit has come upon you; and you shall be witnesses to Me in Jerusalem, and in all Judea and Samaria, and to the end of the earth."

Lesson to Learn

Josiah was the last good king of Judah. He gave it his best shot despite knowing that the nation would be judged after his death. Like Josiah, we must do our best while we are alive on this earth. Yes, the world is headed for a bad finish. Yes, the world is against God. However, we are to seek to spread the gospel to all the nations regardless of how bad things may get. We are not to have a fatalistic attitude. We are to be salt and light to this world because in the end it really does matter.

Questions to Ponder

1. No one can control the time in which he or she was born. Josiah was born at a bad time to be a Jewish king. The die had already been cast. Judgment was imminent. Do you have a hard time accepting the environment into which you were born? Do you harbor resentment toward previous generations of your family?

2. Despite being dealt a losing hand, Josiah decided to make the best of things. As such, he guided his life by scripture. The discovery of the book of the law in the temple was a very pivotal time in his life. Are you making the best out of your situation in life? Are you giving it all you have for the glory of God?

3. Scripture records how Josiah grew closer to God as he aged. There were acts of righteousness that came after he began to seek the Lord. Even though he was playing on the losing team, he still took seriously his walk with God. His actions cut across the grain of a wayward nation, yet he continued to pursue God. How willing are you to provide righteous leadership to those who may not share your values? Is your walk with God manifesting itself in outward actions?

Conclusion

The treatment of Native Americans is a sore spot in the annals of the history of the United States. Many believed that it was destiny that the American pioneers of European descent would eventually occupy all the land between the two oceans on the North American continent. This belief was encapsulated in the nineteenth century with the phrase "manifest destiny."[69] Newspaper editor Horace Greeley added fuel to the fire when he popularized the saying, "Go west, young man."[70] There was so much land to be had, and the immigrants were arriving from Europe by the droves. However, there was a big problem. The American West was still populated with Native Americans who viewed life and land ownership differently. Therefore, the United States government entered all sorts of treaties with the various tribes in order to make way for the westward expansion. To say the least, the whole process was very messy, and the treaties were not always honored. Eventually, the western tribes were subjugated and forced to live on reservations. However, the plight of one tribe captivated the heart of the nation.

---

[69] https://www.britannica.com/event/Manifest-Destiny.

[70] https://www.britannica.com/biography/Horace-Greeley.

As the Nez Perce tribe of Oregon was in the process of leaving their land and heading to a reservation in Idaho, armed conflict broke out with the local settlers. Knowing that victory was impossible, Chief Joseph of the Nez Perce engaged in a 1,400-mile retreat with seven hundred people, of whom only two hundred were warriors.[71] His hope was to reach Canada, where he could get asylum for his people. Despite being hunted by two thousand soldiers and their Indian cohorts, Chief Joseph was able to continue his trek for three months until he was forced to surrender when he was only forty miles from the Canadian border. His speech of surrender is considered one of the saddest, yet most poignant speeches ever made. Here is what he said on October 5, 1877:

> I am tired of fighting. Our chiefs are killed. Looking Glass is dead. Toohoolhoolzote is dead. The old men are all dead. It is the young men who say, "Yes" or "No." He who led the young men [Olikut] is dead. It is cold, and we have no blankets. The little children are freezing to death. My people, some of them, have run away to the hills, and have no blankets, no food. No one knows where they are—perhaps freezing to death. I want to have time to look for my children and see how many of them I can find. Maybe I shall find them among the dead. Hear me, my chiefs!

---

[71] https://www.biography.com/people/chief-joseph-9358227.

I am tired. My heart is sick and sad. From where
the sun now stands I will fight no more forever.[72]

The Nez Perce experienced total defeat, and it was
heartbreaking. Every strata of society suffered. The young and
the old all experienced the harsh reality of defeat. The same was
true with the people of Judah. Babylon took their wealth. Babylon
destroyed their city and temple. They even deported the best and
the brightest back to Babylon. The last king of Judah, Zedekiah,
was also taken to Babylon as a mutilated man.

You Can Learn a Lot from a King

The tale of the kings of Judah is both encouraging and
disturbing. These Jewish monarchs held the future of the Davidic
dynasty in their hands. The welfare of the nation depended
upon their fidelity to God. However, their successes were greatly
outnumbered by their failures. So great were their sins that God
literally had to uproot them out of the Promised Land. The lives
of these kings reveal the true depravity of the human heart. On a
positive note, their times of desperation provide a good road map
for how to connect with God. No other people on the face of the
earth have endured as much blessing and as much turmoil as the
Jewish nation. As we think back on the history of the kings of
Judah, here is a brief summation of some of their highlights and
their lowlights.

---

[72] https://www.biography.com/news/chief-joseph-quotes-surrender-speech.

Importance of Wise Counselors

The people you allow to give you advice says a lot about your heart. Rehoboam listened to the foolhardy advice of his young counselors, and the result was a divided kingdom. Joash had the extreme fortune to have a godly advisor like Jehoiada. So long as Jehoiada lived, Joash did right. After Jehoiada died, Joash followed the advice of ungodly counselors, and the result was disastrous. Hezekiah had the great prophet Isaiah as his sage. Isaiah's words to the king were both comforting and convicting. However, Hezekiah heeded Isaiah even when the news was not in his favor. Remember, no person knows it all. Everyone needs help. Make sure you listen to advice that is bathed in scripture and bears the marks of righteousness.

Condition of the Heart

Proverbs 4:23 says, "Keep your heart with all diligence, for out of it springs the issues or life." Luke 6:45 quotes Jesus as saying, "For out of the abundance of the heart the mouth speaks." The heart is what dictates our actions and speech. Given enough time, what is on the inside will eventually be known on the outside. The hearts of the kings of Judah were eventually revealed by their actions. King Rehoboam is described in these terms: "And he did evil, because he did not prepare his heart to seek the LORD" (2 Chronicles 12:14). King Abijam's reign is summed up as follows: "And he walked in all the sins of his father, which he had done before him; his heart was not loyal to the LORD his God, as was the heart of his father David" (1 Kings 15:3). Even when a king did right, such as Amaziah, scripture notes that the wrong motive for right actions will eventually be exposed. "And he did what was right in the sight of the LORD, but not with a loyal heart" (2 Chronicles 25:2). For Amaziah doing right was the safest option at the time. However, when conditions changed in his favor, what was truly in his heart became known by his actions.

Classic Rebukes

Just because a man became king did not mean he was above a good rebuke by a prophet of God. King Asa took a pragmatic instead of a spiritual approach in order to avoid a war. Because he chose not to consult the Lord, a prophet was sent with these memorable words: "For the eyes of the LORD run to and fro throughout the whole earth, to show Himself strong on behalf of those whose heart is loyal to Him. In this you have done foolishly; therefore, from now on you shall have wars" (2 Chronicles 16:9). He would experience a forfeiture of future blessings and security because he did not seek God's counsel. King Jehoshaphat was rebuked because of his continual alliances with the evil tandem of Ahab and Jezebel. The prophet Hanani spoke these words to him as he returned from a near-death experience in battle: "Should you help the wicked and love those who hate the LORD? Therefore, the wrath of the LORD is upon you" (2 Chronicles 19:2). As King Joash swerved into apostasy, the prophet Zechariah issued this stunning rebuke: "Why do you transgress the commandments of the LORD, so that you cannot prosper? Because you have forsaken the LORD He has also forsaken you" (2 Chronicles 24:20). These kings remind us of the perils of doing things our own way. We stand to lose our security and forfeit future blessings.

Power of Prayer

On a positive note, some of the kings of Judah prayed incredible prayers during the direst of circumstances. In 2 Chronicles 14:11, King Asa prayed this prayer as he faced overwhelming odds in battle: "LORD, it is nothing for You to help, whether with many or with those who have no power, help us, O LORD our God, for we rest on You, and in Your name, we go against this multitude, O LORD, You are our God, do not let man prevail against You." It doesn't matter how much or how little we have so long as we have God. He is the difference maker.

King Jehoshaphat also shot up a powerful prayer as he faced superior forces in battle. He prayed, "O our God, will You not judge them? For we have no power against this great multitude that is coming against us; nor do we know what to do, but our eyes are on You" (2 Chronicles 20:12). Wow! We don't have a clue about what to do, but we are looking to You for the answer. What an incredible prayer of total awareness of and dependence upon God.

Finally, perhaps the king with the most effective prayer life was Hezekiah. He seemed to really know how to connect with God in times of desperation. As he approached a battle with little chance of success, he prayed this prayer to God: "Now therefore, O LORD our God, I pray save us from his hand, that all the kingdoms of the earth may know that You are the LORD God, You alone" (2 Kings 19:19). Hezekiah saw God's reputation inextricably linked with that of the Jewish nation, and he desired that the world would know that the Lord was the only true God. Finally, in a time of personal crisis when Hezekiah was deathly ill, and he was told by the prophet Isaiah to set his house in order, he prayed this brief yet intense prayer to God: "Remember O LORD, how I have walked before You in truth and with a loyal heart and have done what was good in Your sight" (2 Kings 20:3). That's it. When faced with death, Hezekiah prayed an intense, heartfelt prayer, and God gave him fifteen more years of life. Scripture says you have not because you ask not. Hezekiah asked, and God said yes. We can see from these kings that prayer does indeed make a difference.

What Will You Do?

By virtue of the circumstances of their birth, these men were given the title of the king of Judah. They were the descendants of David and the ancestors of Jesus. They were temporarily given a throne that would one day be permanently given to the King of kings. Their character was eventually revealed through the challenges they faced. Their examples are both encouraging and disappointing. It's true. You can learn a lot from a king. Some good and some bad. What will you do with what you have learned?

Printed in the United States
By Bookmasters